Wolf-Dieter Dube
was born in 1934 in Schwerin (Mecklenburg),
Germany. After working as a journalist, he studied the
history of art, Classical archaeology and pre-history,
graduating from Göttingen University in 1961. He continued
his studies at the Zentralinstitut für Kunstgeschichte in
Munich, and in other museums there. In 1965 he became
Chief Conservator of Flemish paintings at the Bayerische
Staatsgemäldesammlungen in Munich. He is currently
Director-General of the National Museums in Berlin. He has
published several books on twentieth-century German art,
including works on Erich Heckel and
Ernst Ludwig Kirchner.

WORLD OF ART

This famous series
provides the widest available
range of illustrated books on art in all its aspects.
If you would like to receive a complete list
of titles in print please write to:

THAMES AND HUDSON
30 Bloomsbury Street, London WC1B 3QP
In the United States please write to:
THAMES AND HUDSON INC.
500 Fifth Avenue, New York, New York 10110

1 AUGUST MACKE *Girls Bathing* 1913

The Expressionists

Wolf-Dieter Dube

162 illustrations, 33 in color

Thames and Hudson

Translated from the German by Mary Whittall

© 1972 THAMES AND HUDSON LTD, LONDON

Published in the United States in 1985 by Thames and Hudson Inc., 500 Fifth Avenue, New York, New York 10110

Reprinted 1992

Library of Congress Catalog Card Number 87–50465

Originally published in the USA as Expressionism

Printed and bound in Spain by Artes Graficas Toledo S.A.
D.L. TO–1754–1991

Contents

2 MAX LIEBERMANN *Parrot Walk, Amsterdam Zoo* 1902

CHAPTER ONE

Origins

THE CONTEXT

Art in Germany at the turn of the century still reflected the political situation prior to the foundation of the Empire in 1871: the separate states had fostered the existence of isolated schools of artistic thought and practice, and trends continued for some time to be geographically diffuse. No national patterns or movements emerged, but there was a large amount of unco-ordinated overlapping. This is all the more apparent when the situation is compared with France, where the forces that combined to shape developments in art were gathered in the capital, so enabling a new style to evolve in a logical and cogent manner. This was not affected even by the defeat of 1871; while the ever-increasing prosperity of Wilhelmine Germany seems to have created a climate favourable to artists like Max Klinger, whose *3* determinedly edifying paintings of historical events and state occasions plunged into oblivion, with the society that admired them, in the cataclysm of the First World War.

Comparison of Wilhelm Leibl or Hans von Marées, however much we may admire them, with Courbet or Manet, illustrates how difficult if not impossible it is for a German to produce 'pure' art. The harmonious equilibrium of form and content, ideally achieved in a 'pure' picture, is all too easily upset by the weight of philosophical concepts, by idealism or Romanticism. This fundamental trait of the German character was to be the mainspring of Expressionism, too; but here the expression was to determine the form, and no longer be obliged to appear in the guise of nymphs, heroes and allegories. The process whereby the colours and forms themselves became the repositories of the pictorial idea was carried to its logical conclusion in abstract art.

The situation at the turn of the century, when the generation born around 1880 began their artistic careers, was shaped by the following factors. In Berlin Anton von Werner ruled at the Kaiser's side. He was the chief representative of a school of artists whose function was to glorify the reigning dynasty and treat such illustrious historical subjects as met with royal approval. In Munich, Dresden and other

7

3 MAX KLINGER *Christ on Olympus*

cities, too, artistic institutions accorded their official recognition to this type of history and genre painting. It was in opposition to this establishment art that the various 'Secessions' rose during the 1890s, the first of them in 1892 in Munich, where the immediate cause of protest was the absolute rule of Franz von Lenbach. There, Fritz

4 von Uhde, Hugo von Habermann, Franz von Stuck and others founded the Gegenverein zur Künstlergenossenschaft ('Society against the Association of Artists'). Their aims were to raise the standard of exhibitions by encouraging knowledge of French Impressionist art, and to promote international exchanges. They made it a strict rule to limit every exhibitor's contribution to three pictures.

Things had begun to stir in Berlin in 1889. A rebellious group of

2 young artists, led by Max Liebermann, participated in the Paris International Exhibition, commemorating the centenary of the French Revolution, which was ignored by official Germany because of its anti-monarchist slant. In February the Vereinigung der Elf ('Alliance of Eleven') was founded, with Liebermann at its head, and included progressive artists of the most varied tendencies among its members,

4 FRITZ VON UHDE *Two Girls in a Garden* 1892

5 WALTER LEISTIKOW *Danish Landscape*

5   among them Walter Leistikow, Ludwig von Hoffmann and Franz
      Skarbina. In the same year a scandal blew up in the Verein Bildender
      Künstler ('Society of Fine Artists') around the figure of the Norwegian,
      Edvard Munch. In response to an invitation from the society, he had
      hung more than fifty of his pictures when Anton von Werner proposed
      that the exhibition should be closed. A ballot was held, and the motion
      passed by 120 votes to 105. The idea of forming a Berlin Secession was
      talked of from then on. When a picture by Leistikow was refused for
      an exhibition at Lehrte railway station in 1898, he suggested an
      enlargement of the 'Eleven', and the Berlin Secession came into
      existence, with Liebermann as president. In 1902 they showed twenty-
      eight pictures by Munch, and in 1903 works by Cézanne, Van Gogh,
      Gauguin and Munch. The Munich Secession was already going
      through a crisis at this period, and Liebermann succeeded in attracting
      the best of its members, Max Slevogt and Lovis Corinth, to Berlin.

10

6 ADOLF HOELZEL *Composition in Red* 1905

In 1893 the Dresden Secession was founded under Gotthardt Kühl. Special prominence was given at its annual international exhibitions to the products of the Arts and Crafts movement. The Vienna Secession was founded in 1897 under Gustav Klimt. It threw its exhibitions and its periodical, *Ver sacrum*, wide open to every kind of new tendency.

The ranks of the Munich Secession split up into new associations, such as the Neu-Dachau group, to which members of the older generation of artists, like Ludwig Dill, Adolf Hoelzel and Arthur 6, 7
Langhammer, belonged. The influence of the Glasgow School led them to discover the hitherto neglected artistic potentialities of the wild landscape of the Dachauer Moor; from 1894 onwards they painted it and its varying moods in attractive, lyrical pictures, in which forms were simplified and colours showed a strong tendency to take on green and yellow tinges. While the Dachau artists were primarily

interested in giving expression to a characteristically German Romantic attitude towards nature, in harmonious 'tone poems', the younger artists who formed the Scholle ('Clod') group in 1899 sought the more striking effects of brighter, fresher colour. Its members, Fritz Erler, Erich Erler, Leo Putz, Walther Georgi and others, were among the regular contributors to the journals *Jugend* and *Simplizissimus*, and their paintings reveal Post-Impressionist influence. By comparison with the older group of artists, their pictures were more solidly constructed, but the principal difference lay in the Scholle group's stronger colouring and two-dimensional emphasis, without either atmosphere or decorative qualities being sacrificed.

Parallels to the Dachau School can be found in the colonies of artists who settled at Worpswede and Goppeln. Worpswede was discovered for art by Fritz Mackensen in 1884. It is not far from Bremen and lies in stern and magnificently coloured moorland. The

7 ADOLF HOELZEL *Landscape c.* 1905

8 PAULA
MODERSOHN–BECKER
*Self-portrait with Amber
Necklace c.* 1906

artists' colony which soon formed in this isolated spot included
Heinrich Vogler, Otto Modersohn and Modersohn's wife Paula
Modersohn-Becker, who was the outstanding figure among them.   8, 9
By the time the Worpswede group held a joint exhibition at the
Glaspalast in Munich in 1895, they had already achieved considerable
public success with their lyrical approach to landscape.

The school which formed at Goppeln, near Dresden, and to which
Carl Bantzer, Paul Baum, Robert Sterl and others belonged from
about 1890 onwards, was Saxony's equivalent of the Worpswede
group. The landscape around Goppeln was also to attract Ludwig
Kirchner and Max Pechstein, in the early years of the new century.

Another artistic phenomenon of the 1890s also had its centre in
Munich. This was the German wing of the Arts and Crafts movement
originated in England by Rossetti, Burne-Jones and Crane, who

attempted to combat the standardizing effects of mass production through craftsmanship. Their theories were propagated by *The Studio*, which commenced publication in London in 1893; in 1895 Meier-Graefe founded *Pan* in Berlin, and *Jugend* and *Simplizissimus* both began to appear in Munich in 1896. These were the origins of Jugendstil, the distinctive German version of Art Nouveau. The principal aim of the movement was to rescue ornamentation from the all-pervading accretions of the past, and to restore its basic components of line and plane to their proper status in stylizations based on pure natural forms. Led by English and Japanese examples to seek motifs in the world of plants and birds, the earliest direction that Jugendstil followed was a 'floral' one, represented primarily in the work of Otto Eckmann, Peter Behrens, Fritz Erler, T.T. Heine, Hermann Obrist and August Endell. From about 1899 this was superseded by the 'abstract' Jugendstil movement. This was led by a Belgian, Henry van de Velde, a musician, painter and interior decorator, who came to Munich from Paris, where in 1899 he had decorated the editorial offices of *La Revue blanche*, the organ of the Symbolist avant-garde group known as the Nabis. He had first attracted attention in Germany in 1897, when he had had a resounding success with his rooms for the Dresden Arts and Crafts exhibition. In 1911 Van de Velde moved to Weimar. From its original base in Munich, Jugendstil spread throughout Germany: Eckmann went to Berlin in 1897, Olbricht to Darmstadt in 1899, Pankok to Stuttgart in 1901, Behrens to Düsseldorf in 1903.

This survey of the artistic situation would be incomplete without a reference to the powerful impulses which reached Germany from France and northern Europe. French Impressionism developed between 1865 and 1875, its leading figures being Monet, Manet, Sisley, Renoir and Degas, and it had been generally accepted in France by 1890. Although the German painters Liebermann, Corinth and Slevogt went to France during these years, they did not really encounter Impressionism itself, but studied in galleries and academies, and were attracted by the Barbizon School and the Dutch landscape artists Johan Jongkind and Joseph Israels. It was not until the great exhibitions of the French Impressionists in Berlin, Dresden and Munich at the beginning of the new century that their work really became known in Germany. The lateness of the encounter made it simultaneous with the arrival in Germany of the products of the

French reaction against pure Impressionism, with exhibitions of Seurat, Van Gogh, Gauguin, Cézanne and Toulouse-Lautrec. This Post-Impressionism had a far stronger influence on younger German artists, who eagerly took up its theories and its perceptions.

The most profound influence was that of the Dutchman, Vincent van Gogh. The son of a preacher, he was led to be a painter by his love of the tangible world, of God, and of mankind. His capacity for experience grew to ecstatic heights, and his experiences were given visual form in flame-like lines and brilliant, radiant colours. He involved himself deeply with the objects he painted, and thus destroyed the protective barriers between himself and the world around him. His suicide in a moment of mental clarity, amid fearful sensations of menace, was a necessary conclusion: the writing on the wall for the young artists to read at the beginning of their path.

Paul Gauguin was a different kind of figure. He was a rebel, like Van Gogh, but he was also a classicist. His method of composition in verticals and horizontals on pure planes, inspired by Japanese examples, together with his contour drawing, provided necessary restraint and control. This was his corrective to Impressionism. He used pure colours in the orchestration of chromatic harmonies which had as much spiritual cause and effect as chords in music. His search for myth was a product of his weariness of western civilization. This is the explanation of his flight to the simple, primitive world of the Pacific islands, where some of the young German artists, including Pechstein and Emil Nolde, followed him.

Paul Cézanne was also revered and admired in Germany, as the third great pioneer of modern art. But his work did not have in Germany a consequence comparable to that of Cubism in France. The strictly logical framework of his pictorial construction, engaging both eye and intellect in equal measure, remained in the background as far as German art was concerned. The incandescent emotion of nascent German Expressionism did not foster the sympathy, repose or patience necessary to appreciate the delicate fabric of Cézanne's pictorial organisms. Paula Modersohn-Becker was the only German *8, 9* painter of this period who produced a true response to Cézanne in her portraits and in her still-lifes; and she died only a year later than he did.

Paula Becker was twenty-two years old when she arrived at Worpswede in 1898 to study with Mackensen. There she met Otto

9 PAULA
MODERSOHN–
BECKER *Nude Girl
with Goldfish Bowl*
c. 1906

Modersohn, whom she married in 1901. Although the landscape studies she painted in her first years there conformed in their subject-matter to the work of the rest of the community, they were not intimate enough, 'too poster-like', as Modersohn said of the work she exhibited in Bremen in 1899. The way in which she ignored depth and the rules of perspective in order to concentrate on the picture plane was simply regarded as wrong at Worpswede. In 1900 she went to Paris for the first time and discovered Cézanne at the dealer Vollard's. Here she found an endorsement and justification of her own attempts to join masses and planes in a unity fraught with tensions. She returned to Paris to work in 1903, in 1905, and for a period of more than a year in 1906–07. She was impressed by the Nabis and by Gauguin, who influenced her palette and her figure construction. And finally she felt the power of Van Gogh. 'I should like to endow colour with intoxication, fullness, excitement; I should like to give it power', she wrote in 1907, a few months before her death. Even though the last picture on her easel was a *Still-life with Sunflowers*, this development would probably only have been an episode. For the last wish she had, before she died in childbirth in November 1907, was to see the great Cézanne exhibition in Paris. She had taken only a few years to find her way to the 'greatness in form and colour' that she had declared to be her goal as early as 1898: 'to employ the closest observation in seeking the greatest simplicity is the source of greatness'. Paula Modersohn-Becker did not paint personal confessions or emotions; she was not concerned with protest or with drama. That separates her, as will be seen, from the Expressionists.

When the Norwegian Edvard Munch visited Paris, the circle of Van Gogh, Gauguin and Toulouse-Lautrec had a decisive influence upon him. He sensualized his impressions in paintings whose melancholy and suggestive richness are felt to be typically Scandinavian and were represented in the same decade by Ibsen, Strindberg, Björnson and others. This psychological slant in Munch lends the exuberant line and fragmented colours of his pictures their greatness and uniqueness. But it is precisely the quality which is missing in early Expressionist art. The Expressionists' fascination with outline and arabesque showed something related to begin with, but that derived as much from Toulouse-Lautrec as from Munch. The burdened neurosis of his art had nothing in common with the cheerful optimism of a new generation.

The origin of the word 'Expressionism' has been traced to a wide variety of sources. This is not surprising in view of the obvious journalistic temptation to use it as a counterweight to the word 'Impressionism'. In some eyes it derives from the occasion when the painter Julien-Auguste Hervé exhibited some nature studies in an academic-realistic style at the Salon des Indépendants in Paris in 1901, to which he gave the general designation of *expressionnisme*. Others believe the term originated with the critic Louis Vauxcelles, who described the pictures of Henri Matisse as 'Expressionist'. Yet others hold that the word was used for the first time at a session of the hanging committee of the Berlin Secession, when somebody asked whether a particular painting by Pechstein still came under the heading of Impressionism; the dealer Paul Cassirer is said to have replied, no, it was Expressionism. This tale may or may not be true, but it probably reflects a desire to match the anecdotes surrounding the origins of the term 'Fauve' rather than to contribute to the definition of the term 'Expressionist'.

The first use of the term that has any importance in the context of this book is in the preface of the catalogue of the twenty-second exhibition of the Berlin Secession, held in April 1911. In it the French artists Braque, Derain, Friesz, Picasso, Vlaminck, Marquet and Dufy, normally described as Fauves or Cubists, were called 'Expressionists'. It was probably as a direct consequence of this that the critics used the word again to designate the French artists represented at the June 1911 exhibition of the Sonderbund ('Special League') in Düsseldorf. Also in 1911, the influential theorist Wilhelm Worringer employed the word in the same sense; and in an article by Paul Ferdinand Schmidt, 'Über Expressionisten', which appeared in the December 1911 issue of the periodical *Rheinlande*, its meaning was extended to embrace German artists as well as French ones.

When Herwarth Walden put on the first exhibition in his Sturm-Galerie in Berlin in March 1912, he showed 'Der Blaue Reiter, Franz Flaum, Oskar Kokoschka, Expressionists', with the last term again connoting only French artists. In fact Walden and his periodical *Der Sturm* tended to make the term vaguer rather than clarify it. Walden soon came to use Expressionism as an all-embracing synonym for what he considered to be the European avant-garde. In the end he treated the word as a kind of trade-mark. Around 1918 he wrote:

In view of the blatant efforts on the part of some artistic and literary circles to appropriate for themselves the designation of victorious Expressionism, without having any artistic right to it, it is in the interests of a clear-cut definition of artistic values and artistic development to point out that all the artists who have any major significance for Expressionism are united in one place. That place is *Der Sturm*.

The word 'Expressionism' again appears in a very general sense in connection with the famous Sonderbund exhibition held in Cologne in 1912. The following appears in the catalogue preface:

This year's fourth exhibition of the Sonderbund attempts to provide a survey of the current situation in the most recent movement in painting, which has made its appearance in the wake of atmospheric naturalism and Impressionism, and which seeks to simplify and intensify the forms of expression, to achieve new rhythm and colourfulness, to create in decorative or monumental forms: a survey of the movement known as Expressionism. . . . While the purpose of this international exhibition of the work of living artists is to give a representative view of the Expressionist movement, it includes a retrospective section, covering the historical basis on which this controversial painting of our age is founded: the work of Vincent van Gogh, Paul Cézanne, Paul Gauguin.

Such imprecise use of the word 'Expressionism' served only to make its meaning even vaguer; and the artists themselves, in particular, acknowledged no allegiance to it. The Kunstsalon Cohen in Bonn organized an exhibition in the summer of 1913, under the title of 'Rheinische Expressionisten', which included Heinrich Campendonk, August and Helmut Macke, Heinrich Nauen and Max Ernst, most of whom had been represented at the Sonderbund exhibition in Cologne. This was, it is true, the first time that an exhibition of German artists had appeared with the heading 'Expressionists', but it was not intended as an assertion of any kind of programme.

The first monograph on the subject of Expressionism, by Paul Fechter (Munich 1914), contains an attempt at firm definition. Fechter took it to mean the German counter-movement against Impressionism, parallel to Cubism in France and Futurism in Italy. He referred specifically to the German avant-garde. 'Dresden and Munich share the honour of being the birthplaces of the new art.' What Fechter succeeded in doing was to prescribe limits which are still valid on the whole, but within them the terminology remained undefined.

So contemporary criticism and journalism present a confused picture; but what of the statements made on the subject by the artists themselves? In 1914 the periodical *Kunst und Künstler* invited Karl Schmidt-Rottluff to express his views on a 'new programme'.

> I know of no 'new programme'. . . . Only that art is forever manifesting itself in new forms, since there are forever new personalities – its essence can never alter, I believe. Perhaps I am wrong. But speaking for myself, I know that I have no programme, only the unaccountable longing to grasp what I see and feel, and to find the purest means of expression for it.

In the famous almanac *Der Blaue Reiter*, which appeared in Munich in 1912, Marc wrote:

> In this age of the great struggle for the new art, we are fighting as 'wild beasts' [*Wilde*, synonymous with 'Fauves'], unorganized levies against an old, organized power. The battle seems unequal; but in matters of the spirit it is never the number but the strength of the ideas that conquers. The dreaded weapons of the 'wild beasts' are their new ideas: these kill more effectively than steel and break what was thought to be unbreakable. Who are the 'wild beasts' in Germany? A large proportion of them are well known and have been much abused: the Brücke in Dresden, the Neue Sezession in Berlin and the Neue Vereinigung in Munich.

Thus the artists themselves avoided the word 'Expressionism'. Even Wassily Kandinsky alluded to it only once, in a footnote to his essay *Über das Geistige in der Kunst* ('On the spiritual in art'), where he wrote of 'presenting nature not as an external phenomenon, but predominantly the element of the inner impression, which has recently been called Expression'.

So what is it that in spite of everything allows us to speak of Expressionism, as a coherent phenomenon that still exerts a fascination? It certainly does not lie with the formal manifestations. As Marc wrote, again in *Der Blaue Reiter*:

> It is impossible to try and explain the latest works of these 'wild beasts' as a formal development and re-interpretation of Impressionism. The most beautiful prismatic colours, and the famous Cubism, have both lost their meaning as the goal of these 'wild beasts'. Their thought has produced another goal: the creation, through their work, of symbols for their age, which belong on the altars of the coming religion of the spirit, and behind which the technical creator disappears from sight.

The rising generation stood on the threshold of the new century, full of conviction and faith, prepared to make immense claims on themselves and on others. The programme which Kirchner composed and engraved on wood for the group Die Brücke in 1906, ran:

> Believing in development and in a new generation both of those who create and of those who enjoy, we call all young people together, and as young people who carry the future in us we want to wrest freedom for our gestures and for our lives from the older, comfortably established forces. We claim as our own everyone who reproduces directly and without falsification whatever it is that drives him to create.

With the tempestuous enthusiasm of youth, fired by the belief in a world 'with a superabundance of the beautiful, the strange, the mysterious, the terrible and the divine', this generation demanded the freedom for a new kind of art to come into existence, to be the symbol and the expression of a new kind of human being. They promoted their cause with passionate ardour. The poet Johannes R. Becher, looking back, wrote: 'We were possessed. In cafés, on the streets, in our studios, day and night, we were "on the march", at a cracking pace, to fathom the unfathomable: poets, painters and musicians all working together to create "the art of the century", an incomparable art towering timelessly over the art of all past centuries.'

The spotlight fell on the elements that united the arts, not on their differences and divisions. They might have said, with their contemporary, Franz Kafka: 'There is only a goal. What we call the path is hesitation.'

10 ERICH HECKEL Poster for Brücke exhibition 1908

CHAPTER TWO

Dresden

The revolution of young artists in Germany was led by Die Brücke *10*
('The Bridge'), a group formed in Dresden in 1905. The nucleus, the
revolutionary cell, was composed of four students of architecture:
Ernst Ludwig Kirchner, Fritz Bleyl, Erich Heckel and Karl Schmidt-
Rottluff. The oldest was twenty-five years old, the youngest not yet
twenty-two, and none of them had had any instruction or experience
in painting worth mentioning. The beginning, then, was not part of
a process of artistic development, necessarily leading to the formation
of the group; it was their strength of will and belief in their own powers
that provided the mainspring of the association.

Kirchner and Bleyl had been studying architecture since 1901 at the
Technische Hochschule in Dresden, where they had made each other's
acquaintance in 1902. They began to experiment in painting and
drawing together. Bleyl, who later went on to devote his energies
entirely to architecture, wrote of his early connection with Kirchner:
'We established a friendly relationship at once, and, striving for the
same goals, we quickly developed a deep friendship. We were constantly together, either at the Hochschule, in our lodgings, or taking
walks in the evenings in the Grosser Garten in Dresden. We were
never without pencil and paper.'

Heckel and Schmidt-Rottluff got to know each other at about the
same time in near-by Chemnitz, while they were still schoolboys.
They first met at a literary society. Besides a liking for poetry, they
soon discovered that they shared a love of painting and began to draw
and paint together. Heckel went to Dresden in 1904, to study architecture, and soon met Kirchner and Bleyl through his elder brother.
Finally Schmidt-Rottluff came to Dresden, also to study architecture,
although he only kept it up for two semesters.

There is a memoir of these four students by their teacher, the town-
planner Fritz Schumacher, who, among other things, made a sweeping
reform in the method of teaching freehand drawing.

The restless, searching character that every teacher of architecture recognizes in his students never deserted any of the Brücke people: with Kirchner it took, to begin with, the cast of a rather taciturn bitterness, with Heckel its form was more that of a sustained passion. It is not easy for a teacher to know how far he should indulge this kind of critical restlessness, since it is very often coupled with the purely intellectual gift that goes with an absence of practical creative ability. I was therefore very pleased when I gradually succeeded in directing these restless elements along the path of a purely naturalistic technique of drawing. This did not last long, however: it stopped very suddenly. I still remember the first time when Heckel, who had started to draw a plant in the broad black and white manner of a woodcut, stopped bothering to observe the overlapping and movement of the leaves, and instead got down on the paper something that bore a distant resemblance to the overall form of the object. When I criticized the drawing for its carelessness he invoked his right to stylize. I put it that a person must be able to draw correctly before going on to stylization, and referred to drawings by [William] Nicholson and others who worked in a similar black-and-white, poster-like style, which I sometimes used in order to show that they were based on an exact study of form. But I did not convince him. He said that the only important thing so far as he was concerned was the seizure of a total expression.

Kirchner and Bleyl took their final examinations in architecture in 1905, and then, together with Heckel and Schmidt-Rottluff, devoted themselves exclusively to painting. Instinctively and without any guidance, they selected the artistic stimuli that were right for them. They visited the great Dresden public collections, the Gemäldegalerie for paintings and the Kupferstichkabinett for prints. The director of the Kupferstichkabinett, Max Lehrs, made a policy of showing and buying modern foreign graphic work; the best of Toulouse-Lautrec's lithographs, for instance, could be seen there from 1900. The young artists saw Frederick Augustus II's collection of engravings on the terrace of the Brühl Palace, and discovered a love for the work of Cranach, Beham, Dürer and the early Italian masters, and for the drawings and etchings of Hercules Seghers and Rembrandt. A little later Kirchner discovered the carvings of the Palau islanders in the Ethnographisches Museum and enthusiastically told his friends about them. It was at very much the same time that Matisse was buying Negro sculptures in Paris and showing them to Picasso, who, for his part, had just discovered ancient Iberian art. The coincidence of timing is indicative of the inevitability of this development, which had started with Gauguin and now made its real breakthrough.

The most important stimuli came from the exhibitions held in various private galleries in Dresden, which were ahead of public taste in general. The Galerie Arnold showed fifty Van Goghs as early as 1905, and 132 works by the Belgian and French Post-Impressionists in 1906, notably Georges Seurat, Henri-Edmond Cross, Paul Signac, Emile Bernard and Maurice Denis, as well as Gauguin and Félix Vallotton; also in 1906, the Sächsischer Kunstverein exhibited twenty paintings by Munch. In 1907 they were able to see French Impressionists and Post-Impressionists such as Monet, Pissarro, Sisley and Denis, while the Galerie Arnold mounted a large Viennese exhibition which brought together works by the Vienna Secession, by members of the Künstlerhaus ('house of artists') and by independents. There were 317 paintings and pieces of sculpture on show as well as a large number of woodcuts, etchings and lithographs. The Brücke group saw works by Klimt, Wilhem List, Carl Moll and others. They were already acquainted with the graphics of the Vienna Secession from its periodical *Ver Sacrum*. In 1908 the Kunstsalon Richter put on a retrospective of a hundred paintings by Van Gogh, and in 1908 an exhibition of young French artists including Van Dongen, Vlaminck, Guérin and Friesz.

The restless, searching character that Schumacher observed in Kirchner and Heckel was caused by youthful dissatisfaction with the here-and-now. As painters they could follow a more subjective line than as architects. They brought a frenzied dedication to their painting and tolerated no instruction. They wanted to preserve the freshness and naivety of their sensations, the strength and honesty of their visions. Their self-will and self-confidence, the uncompromisingly high demands they made on themselves and on the world in general, gave them the power to set up their own goals and to reject both traditional ideals and traditional skills. Their conception of art was as 'original creativity', not as technique; their goal was something that they believed could not be taught.

Since their goal was the essence of art, above all form and colour, painting was not intrinsically more important to them than the graphic media; and above all they favoured the woodcut. In their hands its angular forthrightness became an independent means of expression, not merely a substitute for painting. Painting and black-and-white

11 ERNST LUDWIG KIRCHNER
Cover of 4th annual
portfolio of the Brücke
1909

media continually influenced each other. A strong will to express
sought the means that best suited it; it was in this respect that the
Brücke artists sensed and consciously proclaimed their kinship with
the tradition of sixteenth-century Germany.

Nowhere do severity of construction, strength of contrast and an
uncompromising emphasis on plane and line find so complete fulfilment as in the woodcut, a medium whose expressive potentialities
range from small-scale intimacies to the public statements of the
leaflet and the poster. In the nineteenth century, under the strong and
persistent influence of the Japanese woodcut, artists like Nicholson
and Vallotton had restored to the medium its decorative qualities,
which had a decisive effect on its use by serious artists, and on the
illustrative style of Art Nouveau. The first major achievements were
those of Gauguin and Munch, who exploited the medium's potentiality
of expression for artistic, pictorial purposes.

12 KARL SCHMIDT-
ROTTLUFF
*Berliner Strasse,
Dresden* 1909

The woodcut achieved its highest degree of artistic justification in
the work of the Brücke. The solutions it offered to Kirchner, Heckel   *11*
and Schmidt-Rottluff in their search for the most direct and economical formal means of expressing the essence of a subject led to its
becoming their characteristic medium, and from there to its re-
establishment as a major art-form, most particularly in Germany.
Kirchner was very deeply conscious of the significance of graphic art
for himself and his friends, which he defined in the following terms:

> The desire that drives an artist to graphic work is perhaps partly the
> effort to capture the unique and indefinite nature of a drawing in a fixed
> and durable form. Another aspect of it is that the technical manipulations
> exercise energies in the artist that he does not use in the far less strenuous
> crafts of drawing and painting. The mechanical process of printing lends
> unity to the separate stages of the work. The task of giving the work its
> form can be prolonged as much as one likes, without the least risk.

Reworking a piece for weeks or even months on end has a great attraction, making it possible to achieve the ultimate in expressiveness and perfection of form, without the plate losing any of its freshness. The mysterious attraction that surrounded the invention of printing in the Middle Ages is still felt by anyone who takes up graphics seriously and performs every stage in the process with his own hands.

The young artists were left in peace to pursue their earnest endeavours without interference. Dresden preserved its dreamy calm, in spite of the excitement of the successive exhibitions, and left them alone. Kirchner wrote in his diary in 1923:

It was lucky that our group was composed of genuinely talented people, whose characters and gifts, even in the context of human relations, left them with no other choice but the profession of artist, whose ways of life and work, strange as they were in the eyes of conventional people, were not deliberately intended to *épater les bourgeois*, but were simply the outcome of a naive and pure compulsion to bring art and life together in harmony. And it is this, more than anything else, that has had so enormous an influence on the forms of present-day art. Uncomprehended for the most part, and totally distorted; for with us [the will] shaped the form and gave it meaning, whereas now strange forms are stuck on to accustomed ideas, like a top-hat on a cow.

The way this aspect of our everyday surroundings developed, from the first painted ceiling in the first Dresden studio to the total harmony of the rooms in each of our studios in Berlin, was an uninterrupted logical progression, which went hand in hand with our artistic development in paintings, prints and sculpture. The first bowl which was carved because we couldn't find one we liked in any shop introduced plastic form to the two-dimensional form of the picture, and in this way our personal form was hammered out to the last stroke by way of the various techniques. The love which the artist felt for the girl who was his companion and helper, flowed over the carved figure, was ennobled [in] the picture, [by way of] the surroundings, and in its turn prompted the particular form of the chairs and tables from the habits of the human model. That was our way of creating art, in a simple example. That is the way the Brücke looked at art.

This total dedication shone in Erich Heckel's eyes the first time he came to my studio to draw nudes and climbed the stairs declaiming aloud from *Zarathustra*, and months [later] I saw the same light shining in Schmidt-Rottluff's eyes, when he came to us, looking, like me, for freedom in free work; and the first thing for the artists was free drawing from the free human body in the freedom of nature. It started in

Kirchner's studio as a matter of convenience. We drew and we painted. Hundreds of drawings a day, with talk and fooling in between, the artists joining the models before the easel and vice versa. All the encounters of everyday life were incorporated in our memories in this way. The studio became the home of the people who were being drawn: they learned from the artists and the painters from them. The pictures took on immediate and abundant life.

Heckel had rented a butcher's shop for a studio, in the Berliner Strasse, a working-class area of Dresden. The group worked there with the energy and intensity of the possessed. *12*

Reading the concise, challenging words of the Brücke's programme today (see p. 21), it is hard to concur with the opinion that art critics have expressed up till now, that the declaration is couched in conventionally general terms and does not actually say very much. Just as the Brücke set themselves apart from other artists' associations as a serious fighting unit, so their challenge differed fundamentally from the manifestos of others. Here, in Dresden, in the year 1906, the consumer, the person who came to look, was taken into consideration on terms of equality with the artist for the first time. Faith was pinned on the 'new generation both of those who create and of those who enjoy'. Thus it was not for the artists to form cells, but to alter the consciousness of members of the public by forming groups that included them. The Brücke therefore invited the public to become what they called 'passive members'. For an annual subscription of twelve marks the passive members – some of whom were extremely active in promoting understanding of the new kind of art – received each year a report of the group's activities and a portfolio of prints, the *11* 'Brücke-Mappen' which were to become so famous and so much sought-after. Sixty-eight members were recruited in this fashion.

The Brücke circle regarded the multiple reproduction of their work by means of prints as likely to be an effective way of reaching a wider public still. The individual members of the group made very different uses of the method, however. The idea held most attraction for Heckel, who was also the businessman of the group. He always looked on the print as a means of dissemination on a wide front, so many of his woodcuts were printed in very large editions. Kirchner, on the other hand, nearly always ran off his own prints himself, with very few exceptions, and every impression has an individual character. He was not interested in large-scale distribution, any more than

Schmidt-Rottluff, who still refuses to acknowledge any print that does not bear his signature. The fact that the great majority of the people reached by this means were those who were already interested or had been converted – and the situation has hardly altered, in this respect, to this day – does not invalidate the premiss.

The work the four friends did together benefited from the circumstance that they normally split up in the summer months, and were then able to assimilate their individual experiences under the critical eyes of the rest of the group when they were reunited. Pechstein recalled the summer of 1910:

> When we met in Berlin, I arranged with Heckel and Kirchner that the three of us would go and work together on the lakes at Moritzburg near Dresden. We had long been familiar with the region, and we knew that we would have the opportunity to paint nudes in the open air without interference. When I arrived in Dresden and went along to the old shop in the Friedrichstadt, we set about putting our plan into practice.
>
> We had to find two or three people who were not professional models and would therefore pose for us without falling into studio routines. I thought of my old friend, the porter at the Academy – I now remember that his name was Rasch – and he not only came up with a good idea on the spot, but also actually knew of someone, and so proved himself our friend in need. He sent us to the wife and two daughters of an artiste who had died. I explained our serious artistic purpose to the lady. She called on us in our shop in the Friedrichstadt, and since the milieu she found there was familiar to her she agreed to her daughters going to Moritzburg with us. We were lucky with the weather, too: not a single rainy day. From time to time there was a horse fair in Moritzburg. I portrayed the crowd thronging about the glistening bodies of the animals in a painting and a large number of sketches.
>
> Otherwise, we artists set out early every morning, laden with our equipment, followed by the models with bags full of good things to eat and drink. We lived in complete harmony, we worked and we went swimming. If we needed a male model to set off the girls, one of us would leap into the breach. Now and again the girls' mother would put in an appearance, like an anxious hen, to make sure that the ducklings she had hatched were coming to no harm on the pond of life. She always went back to Dresden with a light heart and thoroughly impressed by our work. Each of us executed a great number of drawings and paintings.

They made sketches without number to record their impressions, quickly dashed down on their drawing-pads or engraved in drypoint.

13 ERICH HECKEL
Invitation to Brücke exhibition
1912

Watercolour also had an important role to play in this, and they soon became highly proficient in the medium. The essential thing was spontaneity of expression, and this was to be derived from natural attitudes, as much like chance ones as possible. Therefore, from the very first, they practised drawing nudes quickly, with the models frequently changing their poses. When they subsequently went on to transfer the material to woodblock and canvas, the proportions and artistic arrangement were preserved.

Their principal subjects were the nude in interiors and, above all, in landscape settings, as just one form of natural life. In addition, the circus and the music-hall were manifestations of life lived at a higher intensity. Both forms of life, the natural and the artificial were ways by which fossilized bourgeois attitudes could be overcome, ways to the 'new human being'. In order to represent this goal as clearly as possible, the individual was subordinated to the general. The titles of pictures avoid references to names or personal attributes, even in the case of portraits, and relate to circumstances instead.

In accordance with the intention, expressed in the Brücke programme, of bringing together everyone who shared their aims, the
group could not and did not remain limited to the four friends who
originally formed it. When Nolde exhibited at the Galerie Arnold in
Dresden in 1906, the group immediately sent him an invitation to
join them, although he was much older than any of them. The letter
was written by Schmidt-Rottluff:

> To go straight to the point, the local group of artists called the Brücke
> would reckon it a high honour to be able to welcome you as a member.
> Of course, you will know as little about the Brücke as we knew about
> you before your exhibition at Arnold's. Now, one of the aims of the
> Brücke is to attract all the revolutionary and fermenting elements to
> itself – that's the meaning of the name, Brücke. The group also arranges
> several exhibitions a year, which it sends on tour in Germany, so that
> individuals are relieved of commercial bothers. Another of our aims is
> getting an exhibition room of our own – an ideal at the moment, since
> we haven't yet got the money. – Now, dear Herr Nolde, think as you
> like and what you like, we hope this offer is the proper price for your
> tempests of colour. With deepest respect and homage, the artists of the
> Brücke.

Nolde was a member for a year and a half.

In 1906 the Swiss artist Cuno Amiet and the Finn Axel Gallén-
Kallela joined the Brücke for a time. Both about the same age as
Nolde, the contact with them was made through exhibitions, and
their participation in the group's activities was also confined to showing
in the Brücke exhibitions.

In the summer of the same year, 1906, Heckel met Max Pechstein.
Pechstein described the meeting:

> I was commissioned to do a ceiling-painting and an altar-painting for
> the Saxon pavilion at the third German Arts and Crafts exhibition, by
> the architects Lossow and Max Hans Kühne, and a few smaller ceiling-
> paintings for Professor Wilhelm Kreis. In the large ceiling-piece I varied
> my tulips. But when I went in before the opening I was horrified to see
> that the fiery red had been toned down with streaks of grey, sobered up,
> adapted to conventional tastes. The scaffolding had gone; I stood help-
> lessly on the floor, unable to reach my work. I gave furious vent to my
> feelings. Suddenly there was someone at my side, seconding my
> vituperations. It was Erich Heckel, who was still working for Kreis at
> that time. Joyfully we discovered our total accord in the drive towards

liberation, an art which charged forwards, unimpeded by conventions. And that was how I joined the Brücke.

In 1908 Franz Nölken, born in Hamburg in 1884, joined the Brücke for a short time, but soon left for Paris, to study with Matisse.

When the paintings that Nolde, Pechstein and others submitted to the 1910 exhibition of the Berlin Secession were rejected, they founded the Neue Sezession, with Pechstein as president, and gave joint exhibitions with the other members of the Brücke. Otto Mueller, one of the 'rejected artists', joined the Brücke as a result.

Finally the Brücke gained one more new member in 1911, the Prague artist Bohumil Kubišta, but their contact with him never became particularly close. While it is true that the artistic achievement of the Brücke was on the whole confined to the members who constantly worked together, their attempts to attract foreign artists to join the group are worthy of note. In 1908, for instance, Kees van Dongen was also invited to exhibit with them. In every case the need to unify the progressive forces in art was given precedence over the criterion of individual artistic merit.

Although the Brücke continued to operate as a group after 1911, the six years spent working together had allowed the artists' personalities to develop to the stage where each of them increasingly began to go his own way. Their individual reactions to the new situation differed. The confidence they now felt in their artistic abilities is also illustrated by Kirchner and Pechstein's founding of the MUIM Institute (from the initials of the German words meaning 'modern instruction in painting'); the school was, however, a complete failure.

General recognition of the Brücke's achievement was finally confirmed at the Sonderbund exhibition in Cologne in 1912, where contemporary French and German art was shown side by side. Heckel and Kirchner were further commissioned to decorate the interior of a chapel for the occasion, and this attracted a great deal of attention.

As the need for a severance of their artistic and personal relationships became more obvious, the group tried at first to counteract it, by deciding to withdraw from the Berlin Neue Sezession. Pechstein, who disagreed with this decision, left the group. The plan to publish the *Chronik der Künstlergruppe Brücke* was intended to serve the same purpose. The text was written by Kirchner. Heckel later explained: 'His text was not in accordance with the facts, either in Schmidt-

15

14 ERNST LUDWIG KIRCHNER
Catalogue title woodcut 1912

15 ERNST LUDWIG KIRCHNER Title woodcut
for *Chronik der Künstlergruppe Brücke* 1913

Rottluff's view, or in Mueller's, or in mine, nor did it correspond to
our rejection of programmes in general, so we decided not to publish
the *Chronik*'. In May 1913 printed cards announcing the group's
dissolution were sent to the passive members. But blaming the break-
up of the group on Kirchner's text for the *Chronik* was nothing but an
excuse. All of them were harder hit than they would admit by the
realization that their youthful ideal of friendship would not be able to
hold its own in the future. Kirchner wrote in 1919: 'As the Brücke
never had anything to do with my artistic development, any mention
of it in an article on my work is superfluous.' But in 1926 he began to
16   paint *A Group of Artists*, in which he represented himself and his
friends, an almost desperate appeal to the friendship of the Brücke.
In 1947, thirty-four years after the breach, Heckel made lithographed
portraits of his friends from memory.

34

16 ERNST LUDWIG KIRCHNER *A Group of Artists* 1926

But the group had achieved its purpose by 1913: together they had created a new German art. Thereafter their strong personalities were able to develop according to their individual dictates.

ERNST LUDWIG KIRCHNER

Kirchner is the most important and the most gifted of the members of the Brücke, the one possessing the boldest genius and the most strongly developed urge to experiment, as well as a restlessness that continually drove him to explore new possibilities. Expression was so vital to his nature that it imposed attitudes that set his personal life and his art at the gravest risk; he remained an outcast, a solitary pursuing his dream of painting.

He was enormously attractive to look at: tall, slim, with dark wavy hair and a refined face with a narrow, high-bridged nose and full, well-
27   cut mouth. We know him from the many self-portraits which he did at every stage of his career, in every medium. People were fascinated by Kirchner; as a young man his exuberant laugh was infectious, but already he aroused unease in some of his colleagues. He was enthusiastic, impetuous and passionate, but also distrustful and easily offended; and he did not forget slights.

His hypersensitivity was coupled with an insatiable passion for work, amounting to an obsession, which never allowed him to rest for an instant; his pencil was never still, no matter where he was, at home, in cafés, on the beach or in the cinema.

He did masterly drawings in crayon, on what were often very large sheets of cardboard, and developed a very personal style in water-colour; his prints, woodcuts, etchings and lithographs represent, in both numbers and quality, a towering peak in the art of the twentieth century. He painted over a thousand pictures and found time to undertake the interior decoration of houses and chapels; his own studios were riots of the imagination, bright with batik and embroidery, his paintings hanging on the walls above hand-carved furniture and wood sculptures.

14   He made the woodblocks for the Brücke posters and catalogues, and even at the very end designed the layout of the *Chronik*, integrating the text with engraved illustrations and including a woodcut
15   title page. For Georg Heym's *Umbra vitae* his illustrations included the woodcuts for the cover and an etched portrait of the poet. He also took charge of the design of books about his own work, and indeed acted

36

as a masterly interpreter of his own art on occasions, in a series of critical studies, expositions and apologias.

If the poet Heym seemed to his friends in Berlin to be the incarnation of the new, Expressionist poetry, the same could be said of Kirchner in the field of the visual arts. His own relationship to Heym was perhaps the closest of any; he experienced an almost compulsive love and veneration for him and an intense concern for his work, although he never actually met him. Kirchner had an astonishing way of penetrating to the heart of a matter, of seizing upon the salient point, so it seems inevitable that he should unhesitatingly have recognized the important talents in poetry, too: Heym, Sternheim, Alfred Döblin. He painted portraits of all of them at about the time of the First World War, as of many other people, such as the architect Van de Velde, the important Frankfurt art dealer Schames, the psychologist Binswanger and the archaeologist Botho Gräf. To Kirchner drawing (*zeichnen*) was really showing (*zeigen*); his own time is made visible in his pictures, where it survives to astonish and disturb posterity. *26*

Kirchner began his studies at the Technische Hochschule in Dresden in 1901, then went to Munich for two semesters in 1903–04; there he attended Wilhelm von Debschitz's and Hermann Obrist's art school where he got to know the Jugendstil at its best. The modern instruction in arts and crafts at the Munich school anticipated the syllabus of the Bauhaus in many respects. Although the relationship could not become a very deep one during Kirchner's short stay in Munich, yet he must have received a lasting impression from the school, and above all from the writings of Obrist, which amount to a survey of the art of the new century. Obrist's claims to give 'a deepened expression and intensification of the essence, instead of a hasty impression', and to apprehend art as 'intensified, poetic life', were the younger man's own longings and aspirations.

Kirchner saw exhibitions in Munich that forced him to clarify his own views, such as the summer exhibitions of the Munich Secession, which left him with a feeling of dissatisfaction. His sympathies were more strongly aroused by an exhibition of Belgian and French Post-Impressionists in December 1903, put on by one of the numerous groups of artists in Munich, the Phalanx, which was led by Kandinsky. The exhibits included paintings and graphics by Signac, Toulouse-Lautrec, Vallotton, Van Rysselberghe, Van Gogh and others, and their influence is perceptible in the work of the next few years.

Kirchner looked back on his time in Munich in 1937, in a letter to Curt Valentin:

Did you know that in 1900 I had the bold idea of renewing German art? Yes, I did: it came to me at an exhibition of the Munich Secession in Munich, where the pictures made the deepest impression on me because of the insignificance of their content and execution and because of the total lack of public interest. Indoors, these pale, bloodless, lifeless slices of studio bacon; outdoors, colourful, flowing, real life in sunshine and excitement. . . . Why wouldn't the worthy gentlemen of the Secession paint this life with blood in its veins? They didn't see it, they couldn't, because it moved, and if they took it into their studios it would become posture and not life. And I felt an urging inside me, '*You* try it'; and I did, and I still do.

First of all I needed to invent a technique of grasping everything while it was in motion, and it was Rembrandt's drawings in the Kupferstich-kabinett in Munich that showed me how. I practised seizing things quickly in bold strokes, wherever I was, walking and standing still, and at home I made larger drawings from memory and in this way I learned how to depict movement itself, and I found new forms in the ecstasy and haste of this work, which, without being naturalistic, yet represented everything I saw and wanted to represent in a larger and clearer way. And to this form was added pure colour, as pure as the sun generates it. An exhibition of French Neo-Impressionists caught my attention; I found the drawing weak, but I studied the theory of colour based on optics and came to the opposite conclusion, namely, that non-complementary colours and the complementaries themselves should be generated by the eye, in line with Goethe's theory. It makes pictures much more colourful. Making woodcuts, which I'd learnt as a fifteen-year-old from my father, helped me to stabler and simpler forms; and armed in this way I returned to Dresden.

Kirchner took his final examinations at the Technische Hochschule in 1905. He was now free to devote himself entirely to artistic creation in the company of his friends. He took his subjects from the world around him: urban views, landscapes, portraits of himself and of his companions, later circus and music-hall scenes, but first and foremost the naked human body. One of the earliest oil-paintings which can be dated with certainty is the *Lake in the Park* of 1906. It reveals clearly the influence of the Post-Impressionists and Van Gogh. After the painting of the Secession, the bright pure colours, which he adopted because he felt them to be necessary, must have amounted on their own to a

17

17 ERNST LUDWIG KIRCHNER *Lake in the Park* 1906

powerful liberation. The uncompromising adherence to the picture plane, the two-dimensionalism, is a remarkable feature. This was a principle to which the Brücke artists were to remain committed. Throughout his life Kirchner himself denied any direct influences, which seemed to him, with his exaggerated craving for freedom, to be the equivalent of dependence. But he assimilated influences from his friends with astonishing speed, and they reappear in his work as something quite unmistakably his own.

He now tackled the problem of form, in an amazingly logical fashion. The steady rhythms of his brushwork became more forceful in 1907, and the strokes grew longer, matching the excitement of the forms. By 1908 his paint was churning, impasted, breaking out in a *furioso*. Kirchner travelled to the sea for the first time, to the Baltic island of Fehmarn. The strong impression that the sea made upon him

18 ERNST LUDWIG KIRCHNER *Three Bathers by the Moritzburg Lakes* 1909

is evident in his work; and he brought to the observation of nature a comprehension quite personal to himself.

Kirchner was now developing his unique calligraphy, to which he gave the name of 'hieroglyphs' in 1920. 'Hieroglyphs in the sense that they represent natural forms in simplified, two-dimensional forms and suggest their meaning to the onlooker. Feeling constantly forms new hieroglyphs, which emerge from what is at first sight a confused mass of lines, and become almost geometrical symbols.' Kirchner's meaning is illustrated by the etching, *Three Bathers by the Moritzburg Lakes*, and the oil-painting, *Tramlines in Dresden*, both of 1909. Such strong affirmation in the art of omission is an indication of the advances the artist had made in a few short years. His artistic drive was all in the direction of simplicity and expansive two-dimensionalism, of clear outline and pure planes of colour. Compositions like the lithograph *Rumanian Artiste* of 1910 display clear legibility and an emphasis on horizontals and verticals.

18
19
20

40

19
ERNST LUDWIG
KIRCHNER
*Tramlines
in Dresden*
1909

20
ERNST LUDWIG
KIRCHNER
*Rumanian
Artiste* 1910

Encouraged by Heckel, Kirchner began to carve in wood, figures reminiscent of African sculpture, and this put plasticity back in his style, even in his painting, for all its two-dimensionalism. He was gaining in technical experience, too. In 1910 he got to know Mueller, who taught him the use of distemper, which enabled him to work more rapidly on larger surfaces; he also tried mixing petrol into his oil paints, so that when applied thinly they dried quickly to a matt finish.

28 Kirchner was now equipped with the means to produce his first great masterpieces. In a painting like *Semi-nude Woman with Hat* his style reached what the dealers would call international status. Kirchner compensated for the nervous abruptness of his essentially large-scale, mural-like handling by a cleverly chosen, narrow scale of colour. He took his paint directly from pots, rather than from a palette; in pictures that look like engravings painted in oils, he invented a colouring without precedent in the history of art. His harmonizing of red with blue, of black with purple and red, of madder with brown and cobalt blue, of two kinds of green, of yellow and ochre, is newer, and perhaps more significant artistically than in the case of Nolde, and is no less original than in the rather different case of Matisse. The intelligent but simple organization of a few colour shades betrays a high degree of artistic economy unconnected with parsimony.

The year 1911 saw Kirchner and his friends moving to Berlin, the only truly metropolitan city in the German Empire. Kirchner was now in full command of his technique; he was like a panther ready to spring; he only needed to set to work. His style in this period represents a unique concord between psyche and material. Kirchner's artistic sensibilities, always stimulated by movement, were caught up into the breathtaking dynamism of the city, which was immeasurably greater than anything he had known before. In an extraordinary extension of his capabilities, Kirchner discovered new pictorial methods, unique to himself, and was the first to express the experience of the large modern city in paintings and graphics.

21 An increased sensitivity of form, colour and expression appears in pictures like *Bareback Rider*, of 1912. The tall rectangular format and the section of the circus ring, the centre of which is left empty, are forcefully stated. The girl's clenched left fist forms a pivot, from which the masses are hurled outwards, held by the centrifugal force of the movement. There are parallel brushstrokes, particularly in the outlines, which are laid at an angle to the form; and their colours have

21 ERNST LUDWIG KIRCHNER *Bareback Rider* 1912

not run but remain fixed, almost as in a coloured graphic, so that they act as transitions, making the form mobile and alive. Black is used as a colour, no longer in outline as in Dresden. In addition, the use of grey, zinc green, vermilion and an accent of intense pink make plain Kirchner's intention of giving precedence to colours close to each other in the spectrum, so as to give his pictures a stronger luminescence.

22 ERNST LUDWIG KIRCHNER *Street by Schöneberg Municipal Park* 1913

22   The *Street by Schöneberg Municipal Park* of 1913 captures the desolate grandeur of an urban view. The scale here is confined to silky grey,
29   blue and green; but the *Five Women in the Street* of 1913 appear in black, yellow and green, like fantastic birds in artificial light. The composition is drawn out vertically, the picture surface filled to the very top edge, the foreground and background bound together in a relationship full of tension. The mechanics of the arrangement are deliberately emphasized; colours and forms interlock, engaging each other within the structure like feathers. Yet every individual line is elegant and discrete; the individual form, the hieroglyph, emerges in isolation from the overall form. In the similar composition of the
23   woodcut, *Women at Potsdamer Platz*, the two women stand on the

44

23 ERNST LUDWIG KIRCHNER *Women at Potsdamer Platz* 1914

circular traffic island apparently cut off and yet fully related to their surroundings.

In the summer months of these years, Kirchner left the city for the Baltic island of Fehmarn, where life flowed gently and evenly. In pictures like *Figures Walking into the Sea* of 1912, man is once again part of the natural creation, with a place in the cosmic order, just like the plants and the stones, the waves and the clouds.

24

Now at the height of his creative powers, his senses alerted to the reception of every kind of experience, Kirchner responded like a seismograph to the faintest tremor. The inner tensions legible in his paintings and graphics became dangerously greater. He felt the approach of the crisis which had so deeply disturbed Munch and had destroyed Van Gogh. When war broke out, and it eventually became obvious that it must inevitably destroy the familiar world, Kirchner's strength was exhausted. He, who had experienced the intellectual and spiritual revolution within himself long before, was unable to stand up to the event when it actually began to happen all around him. An inexpressible fear destroyed the human form in his work. Nevertheless, he resisted despair, in the knowledge that he could still serve humanity through his unconquerable creative urge. In 1916 he wrote from Königstein im Taunus, where he had gone in hope of a cure:

> The heaviest burden of all is the pressure of the war and the increasing superficiality. It gives me incessantly the impression of a bloody carnival. I feel as though the outcome is in the air and everything is topsy-turvy. Swollen, I stagger to work, but all my work is in vain and the mediocre is tearing everything down in its onslaught. I'm now like the whores I used to paint. Washed out, gone next time. All the same, I keep on trying to get some order in my thoughts and to create a picture of the age out of the confusion, which is after all my function.

Thus even complete mental and physical breakdown was accompanied by artistic statements like the self-portrait, *The Drinker*, of 1915. 'I painted it in Berlin, while screaming military convoys were passing beneath my window day and night.' The artist is portrayed schematically, gaunt, immaterial. The colours are a passive blue and pinkish brown, but on the facings of his coat and on the floor there are slashes of blood-red. The forms are massive, oppressive, seeming to grip like clamps. The same year saw the production of the series of coloured woodcuts, *Peter Schlemihl* – these were not illustrations to Chamisso's tale, but a personal statement, in Kirchner's own words

27

25

46

24 ERNST LUDWIG KIRCHNER *Figures Walking into the Sea* 1912

'really the life story of a paranoid' – and of the disturbing series of portraits, which seem to penetrate and reveal the sitters' innermost souls, like the justly famous woodcut of the art dealer Ludwig Schames. *26*
  In 1917 the artist's friends succeeded in getting him to Switzerland. Mentally numbed by the sudden removal from the city environment which had been central to his life and work, he nevertheless escaped the madness and death that doctors and friends feared would overtake him; instead, the desire and determination to express in pictorial form the magnitude of the experience that enveloped him gradually won him back to life. He was now approaching forty. The object of his youthful desire, his dream of a pristine, genuine world, of power and strength, was now finding fulfilment in a strange and unexpected manner. What he painted in Switzerland was not Alpine scenery, but his experience of the might of nature.

25 ERNST LUDWIG KIRCHNER
Peter Schlemihl: Conflict 1915

26 ERNST LUDWIG KIRCHNER
Ludwig Schames 1918

In January 1919 Kirchner wrote from his farmhouse: 'There was such a wonderful setting of the moon this morning, the yellow moon against little pink clouds, and the mountains a pure deep blue, quite glorious, I would so have liked to paint. But it was cold, even my window was frozen, although I had kept the fire in all night.' It was
30 not long after this that he painted *Moonlit Winter Night*. In the rhythmic sweep of diagonals across the firm framework of a square, with exquisite silvery chords of blue, pink, red and yellow, he conjures up the magnificent vision of his new surroundings.

In the years that followed, the bold colours of the valley of Davos reinforced the artist's palette. The daring, difficult harmonies of the Berlin paintings disappeared. Full, saturated colours could glow in the pure air. The angular forms of the urban scenes were forgotten, and horizontals and verticals were used to create peace and order. The

27 ERNST LUDWIG KIRCHNER *The Drinker (Self-portrait)* 1915

28 ERNST LUDWIG KIRCHNER *Semi-nude Woman with Hat* 1911

same powerful dynamism still informed Kirchner's work, but it was a movement outwards from within, from his spirit. There was no schematicism and no repetition; the form reflecting the artist's experience changed constantly. Finally, in 1922, at the time of Kirchner's complete restoration to health, a renewed, unmistakable relaxation and stability of form and limpidity of colour became apparent. He had tapestries made from his designs, and these in turn

29 ERNST LUDWIG KIRCHNER *Five Women in the Street* 1913

influenced his other work. 'I see the possibility of a new kind of painting. With free surfaces, the goal I was always steering towards', he wrote in a letter of 1923. An objectivity previously unknown in Kirchner's work now opened up paths for the future.

ERICH HECKEL

'In 1904', recalled Bleyl, 'having taken his *Abitur* in Chemnitz, another young devotee of art joined our circle of friends, a self-confident, self-willed youth with a high, intelligent forehead. He gave the impression of being an ascetic and was filled with enthusiasm for everything to do with art. This was Erich Heckel.' Heckel made a similar impression on his tutor Fritz Schumacher:

> In 1905 I had the opportunity to observe Heckel outside the four walls of the art room. I took thirty of my students on an excursion to see the treasures of the little towns of the Spessart and the Odenwald. In this

30 ERNST LUDWIG KIRCHNER *Moonlit Winter Night* 1919

31 ERICH HECKEL *Flowering Trees* 1906

crowd of lively students, bubbling over with high spirits at all moments of the night or day, his quietness, and the expression in his eyes that hinted at the concealed fires of a young monk, set him apart. It was clear before we reached Aschaffenburg that he was being singled out as the butt that every student party of this kind is bound to have. On the first evening I took some of the ringleaders on one side, and told them that if they wanted to remain on good terms with me they would have to find another target for their wit, as Heckel was not suited to the role. They were obviously surprised, but they promised to behave themselves, and so he was able to go his own way undisturbed in our midst. When we whipped out our sketchbooks, filled with admiration for a beautiful architectural specimen, he didn't join in. 'Don't you think it's beautiful, then, Heckel?' I asked. 'Oh yes,' he said, 'but why should anyone draw it?'

Not long after that, I found him in front of Grünewald's *Pietà*, which was still in the Stiftskirche in Aschaffenburg at that time, and with the greatest of care he had copied the hands that are movingly wrung over the dead body into his sketchbook, which was twice the size of any of ours. Then later, when we were travelling by train through the country-side, where gangs of people were busy making hay in the fields, he suddenly pulled out his big sketchbook again and began to scrawl passionate smudges on its pages. The other boys could no longer contain

53

themselves and a great roar of 'Heckel's sketching' and shouts of laughter rang through the whole coach.

I had said at the beginning of the expedition that I would not be taking note of anyone's zeal in sketching, and I would not look at anyone's sketches unless invited, but there would be an exhibition on the last day, when everyone would have to show what he had done. I offered three prizes for this exhibition, which were to be awarded without any intervention from me, by a jury of the students' own choosing. When the time came I was delighted to find that the boys gave the first prize to Heckel's sketchbook, although most of it seemed rather mad to them. The quiet man had proved himself.

Heckel did not stay long at the Technische Hochschule. He left at the same time as Kirchner and Bleyl in 1905, and almost immediately entered the drawing office of the architect Wilhelm Kreis, where he worked as a draughtsman until 1907.

Heckel, who possessed an almost mystical ideal of friendship and of artistic unity in the common cause, was not only the mediator who held the Brücke group together over the years, but also the practical one who organized their affairs. It was he who found their first studios in a butcher's and a shoemaker's premises, who organized their first joint exhibition in Seifert's lamp factory in Dresden, and who represented the group as their business manager in all dealings with others.

In the early years his pictures are unmistakably the first efforts of an autodidact. The oil paint is used straight from the tube, without being thinned, and applied in a heavy impasto with regular strokes of the brush. The effect is of an over-excitement which is also found in wood-
31 cuts like *Flowering Trees* of 1906. Line and outline are subordinated to the white planes, which stand out in economical, firm, angular, close-packed slices, held in shape by a very small number of black connecting lines. His subjects at this period were mostly figures: heads, nudes and literary themes, reaching a peak in the series of woodcuts illustrating Oscar Wilde's *Ballad of Reading Gaol* in 1907.

Landscapes became more important and more numerous when Heckel and Schmidt-Rottluff decided to make their first trip to Dangast in 1907. Heckel's paintings at this stage still show the same violent brushwork as his friends', modelled on Van Gogh. The pictures are set down on the canvas spontaneously and quickly, with short curving strokes. The predominant colours are saturated reds,
32 greens and blues, as in the painting *Brickworks*.

54

32 ERICH HECKEL *Brickworks* 1907

But Heckel soon recognized the dangers of these wild, uncontrolled storms of colour. This instinctual way, which no longer had the least connection with the logic of Post-Impressionism, could not lead to the discovery of form for him, but only to the destruction of form. The reflection, the intellectual discipline, characteristic of Heckel are already apparent by 1908, in a painting like *Village Dance*. The second 33 stay in Dangast deepened the experience of unspoiled nature; but its effect was shown above all in a new freedom and expansiveness in the choice and representation of subjects. The style becomes more inclusive, softer and more fluent. Strokes are longer and rounder. The construction gains in surface quality, and the spatial distribution in clarity. But the flat surfaces and the illusion of space are still unreconciled. The paint is thinner and more flexible, and covers the surface

33 ERICH HECKEL *Village Dance* 1908

more evenly. The woodcut becomes of correspondingly less importance at this period, yielding, from 1907, to the lithograph, which was in closer sympathy with Heckel's ambitions in painting: he produced no fewer than 135 of them by the end of 1909.

In the spring of 1909 Heckel travelled to Rome via Verona, Padua, Venice and Ravenna. He spent the summer by the Moritzburg lakes and in the autumn went once more to Dangast. The journey to Italy brought him a notable clarification of form. He was particularly drawn to Etruscan art, which left an enduring impression on him. The experience confirmed his choice of severity, simplicity and intellectuality as his goals. One of his happiest and most harmonious paintings dates from this year, the *Nude on a Sofa*. His colours became

35

56

34 ERICH HECKEL *Woodland Pond* 1910

lighter and brighter under the influence of the Italian sunshine. The two-dimensional quality became even more pronounced, although the rounded curves of his outline drawing remained the determining factor which delineated physical volume.

The typical, surface-orientated 'Brücke style' was fully developed in Heckel's work by 1910. The painting *Woodland Pond* shows how the excessive excitability of the early years is now disciplined and under control. Planes defined by sharp, angular contours fit together in a solid, interlocked composition. Landscape motifs from Dangast and Moritzburg alternate with townscapes, nudes and music-hall subjects in a torrential and multifarious output. A lighthearted narrative quality and an engaging delight in visual phenomena make

34

35 ERICH HECKEL *At the Writing-desk* 1911

36 ERICH HECKEL *Nude on a Sofa* 1909

37 ERICH HECKEL *Glassy Day* 1913

their appearance in 1911. The large, severe forms are modified and
36   enriched by decorative details (*At the Writing-desk*, lithograph, 1911).

In the autumn of 1911 Heckel moved to Berlin with his friends and
took over Mueller's studio in Mommsenstrasse. Every summer he
left Berlin for various places on the Baltic – Prerov, Hiddensee and
Fehmarn – until he discovered Osterholz on the firth of Flensburg,
which he then returned to regularly until 1944.

Many of the subjects of these years express Heckel's strong human
sympathies, which, however, had nothing to do with social protest.
The motif always has a personal application. The picture *Two Men*
39   *at a Table*, of 1912, must be regarded in this light. It is a scene from
Dostoyevsky's *The Idiot*, but it is not a textual illustration. Heckel
repeated the motif in two woodcuts, one of which is called *Antagonists*,
which illustrates the general application that he intended.

38   ERICH HECKEL
Crouching Woman
1913

39 ERICH HECKEL *Two Men at a Table* 1912

The Brücke split up in 1913. Even from Heckel's point of view membership of the group had become a hindrance rather than a support. In the same year he had two opportunities of showing his work in Berlin, a one-man exhibition at Fritz Gurlitt's, and a joint exhibition with Vlaminck at I. B. Neumann's.

Heckel's search was for the order of things, for the equilibrium induced by the tension between them. The deliberately angular, clumsy construction which became steadily more controlled and clarified in the large woodcuts of these years (*Crouching Woman*, 1913) enabled Heckel to represent light in the manner characteristic of him. Reflections and refractions are assembled in crystalline forms, as in the painting *Glassy Day* of 1913. The atmosphere is made visible and so helps to fuse sky, earth, water and man in a single experience.

38

37

The outbreak of war in 1914 snatched Heckel from his intense and prolific activity. He volunteered, but was found unfit for active service, and went to Flanders in 1915 as a medical orderly. There he met Max Beckmann and became friendly with James Ensor. Heckel and Beckmann, as well as some other artists, were under the command of Walter Kaesbach, who so arranged the duty roster that every other day was free for artistic activities.

41   In Ostend Heckel painted his famous *Madonna* (destroyed during the Second World War) on two panels of a tent. It became a significant affirmation in his eyes. At Christmas 1915 he wrote to Gustav Schiefler: 'How glad I was to paint that for the soldiers. It is very beautiful, how much respect and even love for art there is in human beings, in spite of everything, and who would have thought that my style, which seemed so modern and incomprehensible to critics and public at rotten exhibitions in the cities, would now be able to speak and convey something to men to whom I make a gift of it.'

40 ERICH HECKEL *Man on a Plain* 1917   41 ERICH HECKEL *Madonna* 1915

42 ERICH HECKEL
Portrait of a Man
1919

The constant strains to which body, mind and soul were subjected
led, in the wartime works, to a certain over-emphasis on feeling and
sensibility. Drawings like *Man on a Plain* have lost something in   *40*
formal strength and clarity, but convey a sense of the nearness of
despair and danger. Heckel returned to Berlin in November 1918. His
intellectual discipline enabled him to regain his formal control very
quickly. The happy balance of intellectual and spiritual forces was
completely re-established in the coloured woodcut *Portrait of a Man*   *42*
in 1919. Line and plane go to inform the portrait with the self-
sufficient assurance of great art.

KARL SCHMIDT-ROTTLUFF

Karl Schmidt-Rottluff, born in 1884, was the youngest member of the
Brücke group. From the beginning he represented the opposite pole
to Kirchner, who made a more or less explicit claim to be the spiritual
and intellectual leader of the group. When Kirchner had the idea of   *16*
painting the group portrait of himself and his friends in 1926, the
tension between himself and Schmidt-Rottluff was at the centre of his

conception. A sketch for the painting in the Staatsgalerie in Stuttgart – an ink drawing executed with pen and brush – shows Kirchner standing in the foreground holding the *Chronik der Künstlergruppe Brücke* and Schmidt-Rottluff advancing on him from the side. Mueller is crouching on the floor behind Kirchner, while Heckel stands behind Schmidt-Rottluff. In the painting itself Heckel has been moved to the position of a mediator, a fulcrum between the two poles.

Schmidt-Rottluff was drawn into the circle of friends in Dresden through Heckel, who had been his friend while they were still schoolboys in Chemnitz. It was he who hit on the name Brücke for the group, and established the contact with Nolde, whom he visited on Alsen in 1906. The Nolde Foundation in Seebüll preserves a record of those weeks in a self-portrait and a portrait of Nolde that Schmidt-Rottluff painted. It was also he who introduced the group to lithography in 1906. But at the same time he always remained a little withdrawn, a reserved, introvert character. He visited the communal studio less often than the others, and did not join in the trips to Moritzburg, preferring to go to Dangast on the North Sea coast from 1907 onwards, often in Heckel's company. Up to 1912 he divided his time equally between Dresden and Dangast. The variety in the scenery, from the tall sand-dunes and the scattered houses of fishermen and farmers to the moorland, fen and sea, powerfully attracted him.

The influence of Post-Impressionism and of Van Gogh brought Schmidt-Rottluff the same freedom in the use of colour as the others. At the same time his orderly approach to creativity, which took him in only one direction at a time, meant that he concentrated on a single subject, landscape. Figures, which occupied so much of Heckel's and Kirchner's output, appear rarely in his work before 1911 or 1912, in paintings such as *Erich Heckel in a Yellow Jacket*, 1908, or *A Break in the Studio*, 1910.

'The bracing air of the North Sea brought out a monumental impressionism, especially in Schmidt-Rottluff', Kirchner wrote in the *Chronik*. He meant Schmidt-Rottluff's thick, impasted handling, and the predominance of reds and blues; the dynamic, vehement brushstrokes with which Schmidt-Rottluff's willpower set everything in motion; a pictorial unity 'which actually lives more through the artist's obsession than through the definition of the subject'.

This was the stage which Schmidt-Rottluff's development had reached in 1907. He spent the two following years trying to bind his

64

43 KARL SCHMIDT–ROTTLUFF
Farmyard near Dangast
1910

44 KARL SCHMIDT–ROTTLUFF
Lighthouse 1909

motifs together more firmly, to find his way to a more controlled expression. His handling became calmer, the brushstrokes grew longer, as in the watercolour *Lighthouse* of 1909. Watercolours like *44* this one, with their relaxed construction, particularly reflect Schmidt-Rottluff's brief relationship with the Fauves. The colours form increasingly large complexes, held together by emphatic outlines. The number of tones is reduced, the luminescence of the unmodified colours heightened.

Instead of covering the canvas with abbreviated structures built up with brush and spatula, he filled it with increasingly large areas of paint thinned with petrol. From 1910, dynamic gestures rooted in strength yielded their importance as the chief expressive medium to plane areas of colour. His preoccupation with the relationship of plane surfaces to each other is illustrated in the contemporary woodcuts, in which details are kept to the minimum, acting as points of reference to establish the subject in the play of black and white. It is the same in paintings like *Farmyard near Dangast* of 1910. The colours are even *43* further from nature than in the work of Schmidt-Rottluff's friends, and are not descriptive. The structure emerges from the boundaries of the juxtaposed planes. Sometimes the discreteness of the planes, and hence the framework of the composition, are emphasized by black lines.

The expressive power of Schmidt-Rottluff's colour was intensified yet again by a journey to Norway in the summer of 1911. In the painting *Norwegian Landscape (Skrygedal)* he concentrated the composition on the centre of the canvas by means of a few red lines. The lines hold fast; the areas of colour are interposed between them, and fuse in an expression of great peace and solemnity. The act of creation through will, which was suggested in the earlier works, is quite explicit here. The observation of nature has only served to enable a transposition to take place.

45 KARL SCHMIDT-ROTTLUFF *Norwegian Landscape (Skrygedal)* 1911

46 KARL SCHMIDT-ROTTLUFF *Summer* 1913

In 1912 Schmidt-Rottluff reached the extreme limit of the possibilities of transposition of the object. It took only a few paintings, like
Houses at Night, to bring him to the brink of a form of Expressionist   *47*
abstraction, which the Blauer Reiter circle was also practising. The
separate areas of colour are no longer clearly defined: they are broken
up in every direction, there is greater tonal differentiation, and they no
longer have only one explicit meaning. It seems only a short step from
here to pure abstraction. But Schmidt-Rottluff was not willing to
sacrifice the power of explicit statement, or to represent an idea
without an object. So the next stage in his development of coloured
planes was in the direction of a more precise definition of the subject-
matter. Landscape now yielded to figures and still-lifes. For a time

47 KARL SCHMIDT-
ROTTLUFF *Houses at
Night* 1912

48 KARL SCHMIDT-
ROTTLUFF *Pharisees*
1912

49 KARL SCHMIDT-
ROTTLUFF *Woman
Resting* 1912

Schmidt-Rottluff experimented with Cubist terminology, as in the
48   *Pharisees* of 1912, but he did not make anything of its possibilities,
since it did not bring him any further towards the definition of space
and volume. Instead he carried over into painting the kind of nude
he had already used in his graphic work, where the contours were
49   fully defined, as in *Woman Resting*, 1912. The brown shading of the
body gives a volume, which seems to be emphasized by the objects
along the bottom edge of the picture. The areas of intense colour
surrounding the figure force it into a single plane, cancelling out the
impression of extension in space.
    In 1913, in a series of pictures of bathers, such as *Three Nudes* and
46   *Summer*, figures and the shapes of landscape are reduced to two-
dimensional symbols. This 'heraldic-symbolic style', forged from the
most careful observation, was simultaneously developed in a series of
53   landscapes, such as *Autumn Landscape*, which represent a peak in
Schmidt-Rottluff's landscape painting.

68

52 OTTO MUELLER *Two Girls in the Grass*

50 EMIL NOLDE *Tropical Sun* 1914

51 EMIL NOLDE *The Dance round the Golden Calf* 1910

53 KARL SCHMIDT-
ROTTLUFF *Autumn
Landscape* 1913

In the following year, 1914, a sense of the impending horror of war turned Schmidt-Rottluff to a new theme. Typically, two women are shown by the sea, in wordless communication, in pictures full of
54 sorrow and silent gravity, like the woodcut *Mourners on the Beach*. The figures, with their overlarge heads and small, expressively clenched hands, move as if in a dream world. For the first time Schmidt-Rottluff's figures show human qualities which are not merely a reflection of the mood of nature. On the contrary, the landscape, which is now represented with more realistic detail, only emphasizes the tension. The colours, predominantly ochre, reddish brown and dark green, underline the melancholy character of these pictures.

In the final months before Schmidt-Rottluff was called up for military service in May 1915, single figures – portraits or nudes that filled the entire picture field – became his sole theme. The necessity of expressing spiritual qualities with nothing more than line and colour threw him back on the African and Pacific sculpture which the Brücke had discovered earlier in Dresden. From it he directly adopted the sculpture's formal immediacy on the one hand, and its plastic isolation on the other, giving his figures a quality as if they had
55 been carved in wood; an example is the 1915 *Portrait of a Girl*.

72

54 KARL SCHMIDT–ROTTLUFF
Mourners on the Beach
1914

55 KARL SCHMIDT–ROTTLUFF
Portrait of a Girl
1915

56 KARL SCHMIDT–ROTTLUFF
Has Not Christ Appeared to You?
1918

58 KARL SCHMIDT–ROTTLUFF
Woman in the Forest
1920

57 KARL SCHMIDT–
ROTTLUFF
*Conversation about
Death* 1920

From May 1915 to the time of his demobilization in December
1918, Schmidt-Rottluff produced nothing but a few woodcarvings
and woodcuts. They include a number on religious themes, chief
among them the series of nine woodcuts on the life of Christ. The   56
experiences of the war made the question of reality less important to
Schmidt-Rottluff, as to many others, than the question of transcendental reality. He first looked for the answer among the ancient
symbols of Christianity, which acquired a new intensity through his
harsh, barbaric idiom. Then in 1919 and 1920 he produced pictures
with titles like *Stellar Prayer*, *Melancholy* and *Conversation about Death*,   57
in which he tried to formulate the violence of his experiences in more
general terms. But the change that had taken place in him is revealed
in all his work. Thus, the watercolour *Woman in the Forest* of 1920 is   58
a new working of the theme that had preoccupied him in 1914, as are
the paintings *Three Women on the Shore* and *Evening on the Shore*, both
of 1919. But the tension that previously existed between the human
figures and nature has been relaxed. The formal dissonances have been

resolved. The dominant element is symbolism in its more general sense, which transcends Expressionism.

EMIL NOLDE

Emil Hansen, who took the name of his birthplace, Nolde, in 1901, was invited to join the Brücke in the spring of 1906. It was at the same period that he got to know Karl Ernst Osthaus, the founder of the Folkwang-Museum. In Hamburg, he gained the friendship and patronage of the provincial Chief Justice, Gustav Schiefler, who had close connections as friend and collector with Munch and with the Brücke, and who later catalogued the graphics of Munch, Kirchner and Nolde. Also in 1906 the Berlin Secession accepted Nolde's painting *Harvest Day*, of 1904, for exhibition. By then thirty-nine years old, Nolde was beginning to gain recognition as an artist.

Emil Nolde, a farmer's son, was born in 1867 in Nolde in the western part of north Schleswig, on the farm where his ancestors had lived for nine generations. In this broad, flat, lonely landscape, continually menaced by the sea and exposed to the elements, the sense of an animate force in nature is peculiarly strong. The natural forms, so easily converted into grotesque spirits and demons by a naive imagination, made the landscape in which Nolde grew up a decisive experience in his life, determining and explaining the greater part of his whole output.

The second decisive influence on Nolde's whole development, intimately connected with the first, was the simple, fundamentalist piety in which he was reared. It remained with him throughout his life. He later confessed to his friend Friedrich Fehr:

> When I was a child, eight or ten years old, I made a solemn promise to God that, when I grew up, I would write him a hymn for the prayer book. The vow has never been fulfilled. But I have painted a large number of pictures, and there must be more than thirty religious ones. I wonder if they will do instead?

This is the reason for his regret that none of his pictures was to be found in a church, and that he had never had an ecclesiastical commission.

When it was realized that he was not cut out to be a farmer, Nolde was allowed to enter a furniture factory in Flensburg in 1884, as an apprentice woodcarver. In 1888 he went to Karlsruhe, where he worked as a furniture carver while also attending the Kunstgewerbeschule (School of Arts and Crafts). In 1890 he moved to Berlin, to work as a design draughtsman in a furniture factory. He did a lot of drawing in the museums, and was particularly impressed by Egyptian and Assyrian art, but appears to have had no knowledge of contemporary art. In 1892–98 he taught ornamental draughtsmanship at the Gewerbemuseum at St Gall. There he discovered contemporary painting for himself, in the work of Arnold Böcklin and Ferdinand Hodler. He was moved above all by Böcklin's allegorical, animistic representations of nature. Nolde undertook long mountain walks and dangerous climbs in search of an intensive experience of nature. The Swiss landscape took on a physiognomy of its own for him. He represented the great peaks as petrified heads on a series of postcards, which were such a success commercially that he was able to give up his teaching post and try to make his way as a painter.

He went to Munich, in the hope of enrolling in Stuck's class, where he might have met Kandinsky and Klee, but his application was turned down. Instead he entered Fehr's school and went to the studio of Adolf Hoelzel, at Dachau outside Munich, where he encountered the lyrical, atmospheric style of nature painting. There followed nine months in Paris in 1899. In the summer of 1900 he returned to his homeland. He spent the following years in Copenhagen and various places in Denmark and Schleswig, and a short period in Berlin, until he settled on the island of Alsen in 1903. Here he wrote: 'I had innumerable visions at this time; wherever I looked, Nature was alive, the sky, the clouds, on every stone and among the branches of the trees, everywhere my creatures stirred and lived their still or wild, lively lives, arousing my excitement and crying out to be painted.'

The inevitable path for Nolde, to whom the cries of animals had appeared as colours even at an early age, was through colour. As well as the Impressionists, he was well acquainted with Munch, Gauguin and Van Gogh when he began, in 1904, to follow the direction they had pointed out, in the use of brilliant colours and spontaneous brushwork. The excitement which gripped Nolde when he worked among the sights and sounds of nature was ecstatic in its expression. He applied his paint thickly, with the brush, with his fingers, with scraps of card, achieving an intensified, expressive brilliance. These paintings have been described as dramatic or ecstatic Impressionism, and their 'tempests of colour' thrilled the young members of the Brücke. Nolde was delighted to accept the invitation to join the group. He needed to quit his isolation and enter a circle of artists who shared his aims. He remained a member for a year and a half and took part in the Brücke exhibitions of 1906 and 1907. He taught the younger artists his technique of surface-etching, which he described as follows: 'Nobody had made the same full use of the properties of acids and metal in this way before. Having drawn on the copper plate and left areas of it bare, I laid it in the bath of acid and achieved effects that astonished even me, full of subtle nuances.'

The greatest profit that Nolde gained from the association with the Brücke was that he learned their facility in woodcut and lithography. But he came to suspect that his young friends were gaining too much from him, and he was not prepared to accept criticism from them. Moreover, he accused the Brücke of having failed to become an alliance of all good young artists, and in 1909 he tried to form a new group, to which he hoped to recruit Christian Rohlfs, Pierre Roy, Munch, Matisse, Beckmann and Schmidt-Rottluff. This project was

59 EMIL NOLDE *In the Corn* 1906

60 EMIL NOLDE *Market People* 1908

as unsuccessful as his attempt to take on the leadership of the Neue
Sezession in Berlin in 1911, with the idea of gathering all progressive
young artists together under its banner.

Taking visible reality as his starting-point, Nolde painted portraits,
landscapes and garden scenes. He tended increasingly to spread his
paint over the surface like a carpet, in the search for greater simplicity
and density of expression. But although he used the language of
Impressionism, he pressed forward single-mindedly to his goal of
'grasping what lies at the very heart' and 'transforming nature by
infusing it with one's own mind and spirit'.

In 1908 he took up figure-painting again, which he had neglected
since his rejection of Impressionism in 1903. In a picture like *Market*   60
People, the brilliant colours are brought together in large areas, giving
the theme a general rather than a particular resonance, an effect
underlined by the drawing, which emphasizes the grotesque almost
to the point of caricature.

79

61 EMIL NOLDE *The Last Supper* 1909

This kind of treatment of his subjects shows an affinity to the work that the members of the Brücke were producing at the same period. But such 'imitation and shaping of nature' was not enough for Nolde. In 1909, barely recovered from a severe illness, he was seized by the longing to depict profound religious and spiritual experiences with contemplative intensity. The first of his religious paintings was *The Last Supper*, the product of memory and vision. Forms are reduced to the utmost simplicity, so that the visionary expression is drawn entirely from colour and light. This was followed by *The Mocking of Christ*, a *Pentecost* and a *Crucifixion*, and in the following year by Old Testament subjects, like *The Dance round the Golden Calf*. The ecstatic abandon of the dance is freely and directly transposed from the artist's imagination in colours dominated by the contrast of the

62 EMIL NOLDE *Hamburg, the Freihafen* 1910

complementaries blue and yellow. The outlines of the large forms are
not drawn but defined by the edges of the areas of colour.

> None of the free, imaginative pictures that I painted at this time, or later,
> had any kind of model, or even a clearly conceived idea. It was quite
> easy for me to imagine a work right down to its smallest details, and in
> fact my preconceptions were usually far more beautiful than the painted
> outcome: I became the copyist of the idea. Therefore I liked to avoid
> thinking about a picture beforehand, all I needed was a vague idea in
> terms of luminescence or colour. The work then developed of its own
> accord under my hands.

Although Nolde spent most of the summer months painting on
Alsen, and needed the winter months to recoup his strength, he did

63 EMIL NOLDE
Slovenes
1911

not neglect the special problems and fascinations of city life. In the
62 summer of 1910 he worked in the port of Hamburg and revelled in its
bustle and activity, which he recorded in etchings, woodcuts and
drawings in brush and indian ink. The etchings, in particular, 'had
noise and uproar, tumult and smoke and life, only not very much sun'.

The paintings of restaurants, cabarets and cafés, based on observa-
tions and drawings made in the winter of 1910–11, are a comparable
record of the night-life of the city, the subject that was to engage so
much of Nolde's attention later on. He attempted to portray the
essence of this seamy side of life by emphasizing its material attributes
exactly as he saw it at a particular moment in time. It is a quality that
distinguishes this group from what Nolde painted before and after.

The next few years were dominated by more religious paintings,
64 such as the nine-part *Life of Christ*, 1911–12. In order to express basic
sensations, Nolde stripped forms to simple elements, and consolidated

82

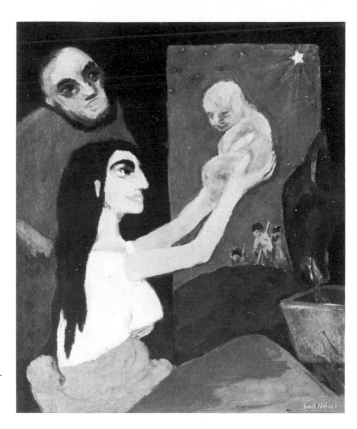

64 EMIL NOLDE *Life of*
Christ: the Nativity
1911–12

colours in large areas. It was his religious pictures which led to the
bitterest controversy. The Berlin Secession's rejection of *Pentecost* in
1910 provoked Nolde's attacks on the Secession, a prolonged quarrel,
his expulsion from it and the foundation of the Neue Sezession. In
1912 the museum in Halle bought his *Last Supper*, but this gave rise to
violent disagreements among the museum's directors, and although
the Folkwang-Museum in Hagen showed the *Life of Christ*, the plan
to show the nine-part work at the Brussels International Exhibition
in 1912 was frustrated by ecclesiastical opposition. The result was that
Nolde became increasingly withdrawn, and from 1913 onwards was
hardly prepared even to take part in exhibitions.

The art of primitive peoples came to have a great significance for
Nolde during 1911 and 1912. It had already been brought to his
attention in Dresden, not least by the Brücke, but it was only now, in
his efforts to express fundamental sensations, that it really began to

65 EMIL NOLDE *Family* 1917

make an impression on him. He began work on a book, *Kunstäus-serungen der Naturvölker* ('Artistic expressions of primitive peoples'), and wrote, in his notes for the introduction: 'The absolute originality, the intense, often grotesque expression of force and life in the very simplest form, that may well be what gives us pleasure in these aboriginal works.' The authentic and original expression of fundamental human emotions was the goal that Nolde, too, sought.

In 1913 he was invited to join an Imperial Colonial Office expedition to what were then still German colonies in the Pacific Ocean, from which he returned shortly after the outbreak of war in 1914. On the one hand Nolde reverted to themes in nature that were already familiar experiences to him, such as light and the sea, which he always 50 represented as primeval energy, as in the painting *Tropical Sun*, 1914. On the other hand he was absorbed by the encounter with human nature and human existence in their original, primitive forms, which he attempted to record in innumerable watercolours and later reworked in more intense terms in woodcuts.

84

In 1916, now nearly fifty, Nolde withdrew to his homeland, western Schleswig. In the simple life of the country he found the relaxation and security that allowed him to develop his work within a particular thematic and formal framework, and to imbue it with a peaceful radiance and stability. He avoided contact with contemporary art, and the first new, major exhibition of his work was not until 1927, on the occasion of his sixtieth birthday. Paul Klee wrote in the catalogue:

> Abstract artists, far removed from this earth, or fugitives from it, sometimes forget that Nolde exists. Not so I, even on my furthest flights, from which I always manage to find my way back to earth, to rest in the gravitational force I find there. Nolde is more than *of* the earth, he is the sphere's guardian spirit. Domiciled elsewhere oneself, one is always aware of the cousin in the deep, the kinsman of one's choice.

MAX PECHSTEIN

The twenty-five-year-old Pechstein joined the Brücke in 1906, the same year as Nolde. His was a many-sided talent. After four years as an apprentice to a decorative painter, he had moved to Dresden in 1900 and begun his studies at the Kunstgewerbeschule. He went in for all six classes in the school's annual competition as early as 1902 and won the first prizes in five of them. As a result he was offered a position on the teaching staff, but decided to transfer instead to the Akademie der bildenden Künste (Academy of Fine Arts), where he remained until 1906.

In that year he won the Rome prize for painting awarded by the kingdom of Saxony. He set off for Italy in the autumn of 1907, spent six months in Paris in 1908, on his way back, and settled in Berlin soon after his return.

Thus he had only one year of close association with the Brücke in Dresden. But none the less the group benefited substantially from his unquenchable vitality, and above all his strong consciousness of the realities of life, born of poverty. Even as a student, he made designs that were always strictly practicable. For his part, the association with the other artists did him even more good than it did them. He was skilful in adapting his friends' discoveries to his own use. While he was in Paris he met Van Dongen, who became a member of the Brücke in 1908, and also Matisse, whose influence is quite overt in Pechstein's paintings of 1911–12.

Pechstein assimilated ideas without any very deep reflection. There is not a single sentence in his memoirs about his artistic ambitions or theories. The bold colours and large planes, which he used in a decidedly Constructivist manner, were the expressive medium of a strong and original temperament. He intensified his coloured reflection of the world, but he had no wish to go as far as symbolism or myth.

Pechstein was not, therefore, one of the leaders of the 'young art' movement, but was, on the contrary, caught up by it and spurred on by competition to do his best works. These were painted in the summer of 1910, when Pechstein went to Moritzburg with Kirchner and Heckel, and then, with Heckel, to join Schmidt-Rottluff at Dangast. By contrast, the works painted in Nidden on the Baltic, where Pechstein went every summer from 1909 onwards – the

66 MAX PECHSTEIN *Before the Storm* 1910

67 MAX PECHSTEIN *Summer in the Dunes* 1911

numerous pictures of bathers and sand-dunes for instance – make a   67
rather superficial effect, for all their beauty of line and decorative
rhythm.

The very fact that Pechstein remained so loyal to naturalistic
representation meant that he was able to act as intermediary between
the new movement and a wider public. He received commissions,
public and private, for stained-glass windows, murals and mosaics;
and in 1909, when he became the first member of the Brücke to
exhibit at the Berlin Secession, he was even able to sell two out of
three canvases, one of them to the influential industrialist Rathenau.
It is true that he, too, was included in the Berlin Secession's rejection
of the new movement in 1910, and became the President of the Neue
Sezession. But Pechstein's allegiances were probably spread too
evenly over every front for him to be the man to give the Neue
Sezession aggressive leadership. At all events, in 1912 he became a

68 MAX PECHSTEIN *Horse Fair* 1910

member of the Berlin Secession once more, and was therefore
expelled from the Brücke.

Success continued to smile on Pechstein. In April 1914 his dealer
Gurlitt made it possible for him to realize a long-standing wish to
travel to the Palau Islands in the Pacific. There he found the integration of nature and mankind that he had previously sought in remote
Nidden and also in a fishing village near Genoa. His carefree life on
the islands was brought to an abrupt end by the outbreak of war
when he became a prisoner of the Japanese. He made an adventurous
return to Germany in 1915. As with Nolde, the assimilation of his
Pacific experiences preoccupied Pechstein for a long time. But where
Nolde endeavoured to trace the primeval essence of man, Pechstein
went no further than ethnographical reportage. Nevertheless, he was
celebrated at the time as the most important representative of German
Expressionism, and named in the same breath as Picasso. By 1922 no

fewer than three monographs and a catalogue of his graphic work had been published. Since that date, however, there has not been another substantial work about him.

Pechstein himself never placed so high a value on himself or his work. He knew his ambitions and his potential: 'I would like to express my longing for happy experiences, I do not want us to be forever regretting. Art has been and remains the part of my life that brings me happiness.'

OTTO MUELLER

Otto Mueller, who had lived in Berlin since 1908, was one of the young artists rejected by the Berlin Secession in 1910. He met the painters of the Brücke at the exhibition of the rejected artists, 'and it was a matter of course that he joined the Brücke there and then' (Heckel). Otto Mueller was thirty-six years old. After four years' apprenticeship in lithography he had gone to the Dresden Akademie in 1894. He left after only two years, however, having fallen out with his tutor. At this period the strongest influences on him came not from the visual arts but from the writers Carl and Gerhart Hauptmann, who were relations of his. Gerhart Hauptmann, in particular, who had once wanted to be a sculptor himself, gave him all possible support and loved him like a son. After travelling in Switzerland and Italy with Gerhart Hauptmann, Mueller went to Munich in 1898 and enrolled in Stuck's class, but remained only a short time. He returned to Dresden, where Marie Hauptmann set him up in a studio.

Until his move to Berlin in 1908, Mueller went frequently to small mountain villages in the Riesengebirge, south-east of Dresden, and on painting trips in Bohemia and the Saxon countryside. Practically nothing of the prolific output of these years has survived; Mueller destroyed his work himself. We know that he had the greatest respect for Böcklin and went to Basle in 1899 to see his work. The arcadian figure compositions of Ludwig von Hofmann also made an impression on him. As well as portraits he painted pictures with titles like *Dancer*, *Venus with Dove*, *Lucretia* and *Goose Girl*. He was also already trying his hand at nudes in landscape settings, and in 1905 succeeded in selling one called *Two Girls in the Grass*.

If Mueller soon turned his back on the anecdotal, literary side of Böcklin's imaginary world, with its one-sided emphasis on classical mythology, Böcklin's example nevertheless did more than merely

52

suggest to him, as to Nolde, the idea of a nature mythology. This is made clear in a passage in Kirchner's diary:

> If one now traces Böcklin's work in Basle from its beginnings, one observes so pure a line of artistic development that one becomes convinced of the painter's great talent. It progresses confidently, without divergence or hesitation, straight from value painting to coloured two-dimensionalism. It is the same path that Rembrandt took, and the moderns, such as Nolde or Kokoschka, and it is probably the only right path in painting.

Mueller remained impervious to the influence of those other artists who tried to develop via the intensification of the expressive content of colour. Even his relationship to Gauguin is confined to matters of theme, to the longing for a simple, rooted way of life. In Mueller's own words: 'My principal aim is to express my experience of landscape and human beings with the greatest possible simplicity.'

He tried to depict the natural concord of mankind and nature. That is the constant, invariable theme of his art, even before his encounter with the Brücke group in 1910, which came at the precise moment when Kirchner, Heckel and Pechstein were about to set off for the Moritzburg lakes to paint nudes in the open air. It is possible that Mueller visited them while they were there.

Mueller had already developed his own generously conceived, two-dimensional style of nude painting by 1910, but the contours were still rounded, gentle, harmonious. Under the influence of his new friends – Mueller went to Bohemia with Kirchner in 1911 – the outlines became more tense and angular, the spatial disposition clearer. As if in order to defend his individuality, he was obliged to clarify his form. At the same time, his nudes and landscapes obviously influenced Kirchner.

'I have always taken the art of the ancient Egyptians as my model, even in purely technical matters', Mueller wrote in 1919. He found in Egyptian art a justification of his own attempts to achieve two-dimensionalism, as well as exemplars of the organization of the picture plane by line and contour. As far as technique was concerned, the example meant the use of distemper to produce a matt finish. This choice of medium is crucially important to the effect that Mueller's painting makes. Its use was only possible, however, because Mueller possessed not only great manual control but also a clear preconception of every picture he painted. Occasionally he used squared lithographs

69 OTTO MUELLER *The Judgment of Paris* 1910–11

70 OTTO MUELLER *Three Nudes Before a Mirror c.* 1912

71 OTTO MUELLER
Couple in Bar
c. 1922

as preliminary models. For the use of distemper prevents any over-painting; it is impossible to disguise *pentimenti*.

The motif of the nude in landscape became a constant theme in Mueller's work. Other themes were pure landscape, occasional portraits, and, from the 1920s, gipsy subjects. Even while on active service from 1916 to 1918, he went on trying to find the purest manner of expression for the same motifs. And yet he was never in the remotest danger of falling into a sterile routine. Representations were checked again and again against the original models, and, when the war made that impossible, against photographs. Self-sufficient, satisfying his own requirements, apparently unaffected by the alarms and upheavals of the age, Mueller went his own way, maintaining, in the words of the *Chronik*, 'the sensual harmony of his life and his work'.

93

72 WASSILY KANDINSKY Poster for the 1st exhibition of the Neue Künstlervereinigung München 1909

CHAPTER THREE

Munich

DIE NEUE KÜNSTLERVEREINIGUNG

In January 1909 a group of artists in Munich announced their common aims of 'organizing art exhibitions in Germany and abroad, and of reinforcing their effect by lectures, publications and similar means'. The founder members of the group, which was called the Neue Künstlervereinigung München ('New Artists' Alliance, Munich'), were Alexej von Jawlensky, Alexander Kanoldt, Adolf Erbslöh, Marianne Werefkin, Wassily Kandinsky and Gabriele Münter. They wanted Hermann Schlittgen, a graphic artist who contributed to *Fliegende Blätter*, to be their president, but he did not even become a member, so the office devolved upon Kandinsky, who was qualified both by his legal training and his experience as founder and president of the Phalanx group.

The Neue Künstlervereinigung issued a circular to mark its foundation; this, reprinted as the preface to the catalogue of their first exhibition, contains the following statement:

> Our starting-point is the belief that the artist is constantly engaged in collecting experiences in an inner world, in addition to the impressions he receives from the external world, from nature. The search for artistic forms in which to express the mutual interpenetration of these two kinds of experience, for forms which must be free of every kind of irrelevancy in order to express nothing but the essentials – in short, the pursuit of artistic synthesis – this seems to us to be a watchword which is uniting more and more artists at this present time.

Before the end of 1909 Paul Baum, Karl Hofer, Vladimir Bechtejeff, Erma Bossi, Moissey Kogan and the dancer Alexander Sacharoff had joined the alliance, and the Frenchmen Pierre Girieud and Henri Le Fauconnier became members in 1910. Alfred Kubin took part in the exhibitions, as a guest. The first of these opened in December 1909 at the Moderne Galerie Thannhauser in Munich, and toured several German towns. The poster was designed by Kandinsky. For the 72 second exhibition, which was again held in the Thannhauser gallery, in September 1910, contributions were invited from Braque, Picasso, Rouault, Derain, Vlaminck, Van Dongen, the brothers David and Vladimir Burljuk and Alexander Mogilewsky, among others. There were also exhibits by the sculptors Hermann Haller, Bernhard Hoettger and Edwin Scharff.

The catalogue for the second exhibition included forewords by Le Fauconnier, the Burljuks, Kandinsky and Odilon Redon. Kandinsky wrote:

> At an unknown hour, from a source that is still sealed to us, but inexorably, the Work comes into the world. Cold calculation, splashes leaping up without plan, mathematically accurate construction (laid bare or concealed), silent, screaming drawing, scrupulous finish, colour in fanfares or played pianissimo on the strings, large, serene, cradling, fragmented planes. Isn't that Form? Aren't those the Means?
>
> Suffering, seeking, tormented souls with a deep fissure, caused by the collision of the spiritual with the material. The Found. The life of living and 'dead' nature. The consolation in the phenomena of the world, the external and the inner. Intimations of joy. The calling. Mystery speaking through mysteries. Isn't that meaning? Isn't that the conscious or unconscious purpose of the compulsive urge to create?
>
> Shame on him who has the power to put the necessary words into the mouth of art and doesn't do it. Shame on him who turns his soul's ear away from the mouth of art. A human being speaks to human beings about the superhuman – the language of art.

Like the first exhibition, the second met with nothing but repudiation on its tour of Germany. One significant outcome, at least, was that it aroused the attention of two young artists in Munich, August Macke and Franz Marc, and encouraged them to make contact with the Neue Künstlervereinigung. Marc joined in February 1911. But the alliance had already started to crumble. Baum and Hofer remained members for only a short time; and Kandinsky wrote to Gabriele Münter in December 1910: 'I must tell you frankly: it gives me no pleasure to think of our fellow members, and I would very much like to leave the alliance.' Things did not come to such a pass at that stage, but Kandinsky resigned the presidency in January 1911. He was succeeded by Erbslöh.

The Brücke and the Neue Künstlervereinigung shared the aim of 'attracting all the revolutionary and fermenting elements' to themselves, those whose works were born of 'inner necessity'. What united

73 WASSILY
KANDINSKY
Membership card of
the Neue
Künstlervereinigung
München 1908–09

the two groups was thus not a formal principle, not a question of style,
but an affinity of purpose. It was therefore possible for both groups to
invite foreign artists who they felt shared their purpose to take part in
their exhibitions. Van Dongen, for instance, was a member of the
Brücke and a guest of the Neue Künstlervereinigung. However, the
Brücke – and Kirchner in particular, with his insistence on his special
relationship to Dürer – passionately denied any imputation that they
were dependent on, or imitators of, the Fauves or Munch. In exactly
the same way, the Burljuk brothers, in the catalogue of the Neue
Künstlervereinigung's second exhibition, rejected the same sugges-
tions, pointing to the ancient frescoes in Russian churches, and all the
icons and folk-art of Russia, as the real sources of their work.

There was however, one important difference between the
Dresden and Munich groups. In the former, as Kirchner put it, 'it was
lucky that our group was composed of genuinely talented people';
in Munich, on the other hand, tensions, soon swelling to ungovern-
able proportions, were created by the different levels of intellectual
and artistic ability of individual members of the group. There was,
for instance, Baroness Marianne Werefkin, in whose salon artists used

to meet to take tea – it was at these daily tea-parties that the idea of the Neue Künstlervereinigung was conceived. She had had private lessons with Ilya Repin in St Petersburg for ten years, and had temporarily given up her own artistic activity altogether after meeting Jawlensky. Since she was hardly capable of contributing anything to

74 the new movement herself, she made great and successful efforts to assemble a circle of people who would be able to clarify the new ideas (*Self-portrait I*, c. 1908).

There were hangers-on like Bechtejeff, who were carried away by the excitement of the start, but never got beyond the level of decoration in their own work and very soon pronounced themselves

75 satisfied with their modest achievements (*Horse-trainer*, c. 1912).

This was the reason why Kandinsky considered leaving, but he stayed on for the time being, because there were no alternatives. The inevitable rupture came in December 1911. The immediate cause was the committee's ruling that an artist could hang two pictures without submitting them to the jury, so long as their area did not exceed 4 square metres (43 square feet). Kandinsky wanted to show a larger picture at the third exhibition of the Neue Künstlervereinigung.

74 MARIANNE VON WEREFKIN *Self-portrait c.* 1908

75 WLADIMIR VON BECHTEJEFF *Horse-trainer c.* 1912

76 ADOLF ERBSLÖH *Brannenburg (Sunset)* 1911

A majority of members insisted that the picture must go before the jury, and in fact rejected it. Kandinsky, Münter and Marc at once resigned. The third exhibition went on with the members who were left. The driving force now was Erbslöh, and it was only personal friendship to him that kept Jawlensky and Werefkin from leaving also.

Adolf Erbslöh had come to Munich from Karlsruhe in 1904, in order to complete his studies with Ludwig Herterich. Like others of his generation, Erbslöh went through phases of Jugendstil and Pointillism, until he and his friend, Alexander Kanoldt, who had also moved from Karlsruhe to Munich, in 1908, were introduced into Marianne Werefkin's salon. The most important outcome for Erbslöh was his meeting with Jawlensky. 'The artists to whom I owe most, the lines, as it were, that showed the direction my own work should take, are Van Gogh, Cézanne and Jawlensky', he wrote later. Like Jawlensky, he confines his figures within emphatic contours, and his sense of colour is akin to the Russian's.

76, 78

77

It was probably the Cubist works, by Braque among others, which were shown at the second exhibition of the Neue Künstlervereinigung, that influenced Erbslöh and Kanoldt in their development of the stiff type of picture construction that Marc called 'such a ridiculous and pedestrian aping of fashionable Cubist notions'.

Das Neue Bild, published by the Neue Künstlervereinigung in 1912, with a text by Otto Fischer, later the director of the museum in Basle, was intended as a justification of the group. It includes the following passage:

> A picture is not only expression but also representation. It is not a direct expression of the soul but of the soul in the subject. A picture without a subject is meaningless. Half subject and half soul is sheer delusion. These are false trails laid by mindless cranks and deceivers. The confused may well speak of the spiritual: the spirit does not confuse, but clarify.

Bechtejeff, Jawlensky and Werefkin protested vehemently against the publication of these views, ostensibly on their behalf, and announced their resignation. And that, in December 1912, was the end of the Neue Künstlervereinigung München.

77 ALEXANDER KANOLDT *At the Eisack* 1911

78 ADOLF ERBSLÖH
Nude with Garter
1909

DER BLAUE REITER

Immediately after leaving the Neue Künstlervereinigung, Kandinsky,
Marc and Münter went to the Thannhauser gallery and asked for a
share of the exhibition rooms. On 18 December 1911 they actually   79
opened the '1. Ausstellung der Redaktion des Blauen Reiter' ('1st
Exhibition of the Editors of The Blue Rider'), at the same time and
under the same roof as the third exhibition of the Neue Künstlervereinigung. Marc had written to Macke on 7 December: 'On almost the
very same day Pechstein, Kirchner, Mueller and Heckel left the Neue
Sezession for similar, and even the same, reasons; *vive le mouvement.*
We are staunch and true and in rather a champagne mood.'

The exhibition was assembled in a mere two weeks, and was therefore bound to make a rather haphazard impression, with works of
rather different standards. Forty-three works were shown, by Henri
Rousseau, Albert Bloch, the Burljuk brothers, Elisabeth Epstein,
Eugen Kahler, Jean Bloè Niestlé, the composer Arnold Schönberg,

DER
BLAUE REITER

Campendonk, Delaunay, Kandinsky, Macke, Münter and Marc. Niestlé, the animal painter and a friend of Marc's, felt so uncomfortable in this company that he withdrew his picture. Marc was devastated: 'A bitter debut for our watchword: Away with programmes'.

The exhibition continued only until 3 January 1912 in Munich. It then toured various places in Germany, and opened in Berlin in March as the first *Sturm* exhibition. Herwarth Walden took it upon himself to add works by Klee, Kubin, Jawlensky and Werefkin, without arousing any objection from Munich, although Jawlensky and Werefkin were still members of the Neue Künstlervereinigung.

That they had done no more than get rid of unnecessary ballast was confirmed by the second and last exhibition that was mounted under the name of 'Der Blaue Reiter', which took place as soon after the first as March and April 1912, in the gallery of the art and book dealer Hans Goltz in Munich. It consisted only of graphic works. The artists who took part included Braque, Derain, Picasso and Vlaminck, the members of the Brücke, Hans Arp, Klee, Kubin, Nolde, Kasimir Malevich, and all those who had participated in the first exhibition.

These two exhibitions were stated to have been organized by 'the editors of The Blue Rider', that is, Kandinsky and Marc. The only indication that the public had as to the meaning of this curious name was in an advertisement for a forthcoming yearbook or almanac, *Der Blaue Reiter*, which was included in the catalogue. Kandinsky wrote in 1930:

80

80 WASSILY KANDINSKY Cover of the *Almanach der Blaue Reiter* 1911

It was at the same period that a wish matured that I had been nurturing, of compiling a book (a kind of almanac) in which all the contributions should be written by artists. I dreamt primarily of painters and musicians. The ruinous separation of the arts from each other and of 'Art' from folk art and children's art, the distinction between 'Art' and 'Ethnography', the solid walls erected between phenomena that in my eyes were so closely related, even identical: in a word, the potentialities for synthesis left me no peace. It may well seem strange today that for a long time I could not find any co-workers or any means to promote this idea, simply could not arouse enough interest in it.

It was the time when all the 'Isms' were shooting up, when there was no recognition for the synthesis of the arts, and when interest was chiefly focused on temperamental 'civil wars'.

Two great movements in painting were born practically on the same day (1911–12): Cubism and Abstract (=Absolute) Painting. Simultaneously Futurism, Dadaism and Expressionism, soon to prove the conqueror. . . .

Atonal music and its master, Arnold Schönberg, who was then being booed in every concert hall in Europe, were creating no less a stir than the Isms in the visual arts. I got to know Schönberg at that time and at once discovered in him an enthusiastic supporter of the Blauer Reiter idea. (The acquaintance existed only in the form of a correspondence to begin with; personal encounter came a little later.) I was already in touch with some of the future contributors. *Der Blaue Reiter* existed as an idea, but there seemed to be no prospect of its taking solid flesh. And then Sindelsdorf cast up Franz Marc. A single conversation was enough: we understood each other perfectly. . . . We were both absolutely clear from the very beginning that we would have to be ruthlessly dictatorial: complete freedom for the realization, the embodiment of our idea.

Franz Marc brought with him a very useful assistant in August Macke, who was then still very young. We put him in charge of the ethnographical material, giving him some help ourselves. He discharged his task brilliantly, and was given another, the article on masks, which he also carried out with distinction.

I took charge of the Russians (painters, composers, theorists) and translated their articles.

Marc came from Berlin, with a lot of material from the Brücke group which had just been formed, and which was totally unknown in Munich.

It was not, therefore, a new group that instigated these activities, and it is significant that no attempt was made to form one. The premisses on which earlier ones had been founded no longer existed. In Cologne in 1912, an official exhibition, supported from public funds, was devoted to the avant-garde: the Sonderbund exhibition. The necessity for the small groups no longer existed. No group even succeeded in contributing, as such, to the Sonderbund exhibition. And when Walden's *Sturm* gallery showed the works from the first Blauer Reiter exhibition, in June 1912, *Der Blaue Reiter* was not mentioned. The title of the exhibition was 'Deutsche Expressionisten, zurückgestellte Bilder des Sonderbundes Köln' ('German Expressionists, Pictures Rejected by the Sonderbund in Cologne').

The almanac *Der Blaue Reiter* was published in May 1912. It contained articles on the visual arts, music and the theatre by Kandinsky, Marc, Macke, Schönberg, David Burljuk, Roger Allard and others, the stage-composition *Der gelbe Klang* ('The yellow sound') by Kandinsky, music by Schönberg, Berg and Webern, and reproductions of works by Kandinsky and his friends, of the art of primitive peoples, of the Far East and of Egypt, of folk art, of medieval woodcuts and sculpture, and of drawings by children, as well as of works by Cézanne, Van Gogh, Rousseau, Delaunay, Matisse, the Brücke group and others. The aim of the almanac was 'that the publication will unite in one place the efforts which are making themselves noticed so forcibly in every sphere of the arts, and whose fundamental purpose is to push back the existing limits of artistic expression.' In this sense the book reinforced a position already widely held, not merely in Munich, and which had already been frequently represented in exhibitions and manifestos.

Thus in a way the almanac marked the end of an association of artists, just as a short time later the *Chronik* of the Brücke attended the dissolution of the group. The fact that *Der Blaue Reiter* has its place in history as a portent of the future is due not so much to the 'juxtaposition of the most varied phenomena in modern art on an international basis' as to Kandinsky's achievement: the breakthrough to abstraction.

WASSILY KANDINSKY

Kandinsky was thirty when he arrived in Munich in 1896. He had managed an art printing works in Moscow and had turned down the offer of a post in the faculty of law at the university of Tartu in order to follow his boyhood dream of becoming a painter. He had bought himself a box of paints when only fourteen in Odessa, and later painted in his spare time while a student. Munich was at that date a Mecca for talented artists from all over the world, and seemed to him to be the right place to begin serious study. According to his mistress Gabriele Münter, he had by 1896 already conceived a specific artistic goal; he told her, when they were in Tunis in 1905, that he had not been satisfied with his painting while he was a student in Moscow. Subjects had troubled him. He had already wished that he could dispense with them. And the experiences that really determined the course he should take had happened in Moscow.

It was at that same period that I experienced two events which left their stamp on my whole life, and at the time shook me to the roots of my being. One was the Moscow exhibition of the French Impressionists – first and foremost Claude Monet's *Haystack* – and the other a performance of Wagner's *Lohengrin* at the Court Theatre.

Up till then I had known nothing but realist art, in effect only the Russians; I had often stood gazing at the hand of Franz Liszt in Repin's portrait, and that sort of thing. And suddenly for the first time I saw a picture. The catalogue told me that it was a haystack: I couldn't tell it from looking. Not being able to tell it upset me. I also considered that the artist had no right to paint so indistinctly.

I had the dull sensation that the picture's subject was missing. And was amazed and confused to realize that the picture did not merely fascinate but impressed itself indelibly on my memory and constantly floated before my eyes, quite unexpectedly, complete in every detail. I did not understand any of this, and I was unable to draw the simple conclusions from the experience. What was quite plain to me, however, was that the palette had a strength that I had never before suspected, far beyond anything I had ever dreamt. Painting acquired a fairy-tale splendour and strength. And at the same time, although I did not realize it, the subject, as an essential element of the picture, was discredited. In sum, I had the impression that a tiny portion of my fairy-tale Moscow existed in beauty on the canvas.

Lohengrin, on the other hand, seemed to me to be a complete realization of this Moscow of mine. The violins, the deep bass notes, and especially the wind instruments, embodied for me the whole force of a fateful hour, heavy with great events. All my colours were conjured up before my eyes. Wild, almost mad lines drew themselves before me. I did not dare to tell myself in so many words that Wagner had painted 'my hour' in music. But it was quite clear to me that art in general is much more powerful than had appeared to me, and on the other hand that painting was capable of developing powers of exactly the same order as those that music possessed. And the inability to discover those powers myself, or at least to go in search of them, made my renunciation the more bitter.

81 WASSILY KANDINSKY
Singer 1903

In Munich Kandinsky entered the art school of Anton Azbe, which was very well known at that date, and there he met a slightly older compatriot of his, Alexej von Jawlensky. Nude painting was taught in the usual fashion of the day. 'Students of both sexes and of numerous races milled around these foul-smelling, apathetic, expressionless models.' Kandinsky often experienced revulsion and felt alien and isolated in this environment. So he painted more at home and in the open air, because he 'felt much more at home in the realm of colour than in that of line'. He stayed with Azbe for two years, failed to be accepted for Stuck's drawing class at the academy, and worked entirely on his own for a year. In 1900 he succeeded in getting into Stuck's painting class, where Paul Klee was working at the same date, although the two did not get to know each other.

Munich was the centre of the Jugendstil in Germany at that time. The idea of abstract art was beginning to develop. Endell wrote in 1898 that artists were 'standing at the beginning of the development of a totally new art, art with forms which mean nothing and represent nothing and recall nothing, which move us as profoundly, as strongly as hitherto only the sounds of music have been able'. So there was vindication on all sides of the goal towards which Kandinsky was pressing, but it seemed to lie impossibly far away. Even when he arrived at the firm conviction that the object was harming his pictures, there remained the vital question of what was to replace the object if it was omitted.

When he left the academy in 1901, Kandinsky willingly succumbed to the influence of Jugendstil. His posters followed the contemporary style exactly. He designed 'reformed' clothing, a tapestry with a motif of crinolined ladies, and patterns for bead embroidery and handbags. He was intensely preoccupied with the woodcut (*Singer*, 1903), but did not get any further than a bold stylization. He had a very high opinion of his woodcuts himself, and showed them at exhibitions of the Berlin Secession from 1902 to 1908, at the Salon d'Automne in Paris from 1904 to 1908, and at the second Brücke exhibition of 1906–07 in Dresden.

81

Post-Impressionism was another starting-point for experiment. Besides landscapes, his paintings in the years up to 1907 were primarily devoted to a romantic fairy-tale world.

Kandinsky had become a member of the Phalanx group in Munich in 1901 and its president in 1902. The group also ran a school, where he taught until 1903. But the exhibitions the Phalanx put on were more important for him, including one of Monet and one of the Post-Impressionists, which Kirchner also saw. The enterprise had to be abandoned in 1904 due to its lack of success.

Since there was little to see in Munich, Kandinsky did some travelling. He visited Venice in 1903, Tunis for four months in 1904–05, Dresden in the summer of 1905, Rapallo for four months in 1905–06, Sèvres from June 1906 to June 1907, and Berlin from September 1907 to April 1908. Throughout this period he took part in numerous European exhibitions with great success. In 1903 he was invited to take over the class of decorative painting at the Düsseldorf Kunst-gewerbeschule. He won medals in Paris in 1904 and 1905, was elected to the jury of the Salon d'Automne, and won a Grand Prix in 1906.

After returning to Munich, Kandinsky spent the summer of 1908 at Murnau, where he and Gabriele Münter bought a house in the following year and where they were joined by Jawlensky and Werefkin. He now began to sort and assimilate the many stimuli that

82 WASSILY KANDINSKY *Beach Tents in Holland* 1904

he had experienced: he named Cézanne, Matisse and Picasso as his chief influences. What he had said of his early days in Munich was true again of this period:

> Houses and trees made hardly any impression on my thoughts. I used the palette knife to spread lines and splashes of paint on the canvas, and made them sing as loudly as I could. That fateful hour in Moscow rang in my ears, my eyes were filled with the strong saturated colours of the light and air of Munich, and the deep thunder of its shadows.

Elemental forces grew in strength in the numerous landscapes, reinforced by Kandinsky's encounter with Bavarian folk-art, which revived his memories of Russian folklore. The pictures are dominated by strong combinations of red, yellow, blue and green. Forms are described summarily by means of planes, dots or short strokes. The motif is no more than the excuse for unleashing the power of colour (*Village Church*, 1908). The material subject is of little importance *83* beside the colour harmonies (*Landscape with Tower*, 1909). *95*

One of these pictures gave Kandinsky an experience that proved that he was now on the right path.

> Evening was drawing in. I had just come home with my paints and brushes after working on a sketch, still abstracted and absorbed in what I had been doing, when I suddenly saw an indescribably beautiful picture, suffused with an inner radiance. I stood gaping at first, then I rushed up to this mysterious picture, in which I could see nothing but forms and colours, and whose subject was incomprehensible. At once I discovered the answer to the puzzle: it was one of my own pictures that was leaning against the wall on its side.

The speed with which Kandinsky now pressed forward to produce results remote from any subject, even in landscape, is illustrated by a
84   picture of 1910, *Mountain Landscape with Church*. The motif is only a pretext. A consistent rhythm is imposed on the natural forms, which are completely subordinated to the picture as a whole. Areas of colour and the forms of the landscape dissolve into structural elements without perceptible transitions. Analysis of the forms of objects contributes virtually nothing to the understanding of pictures like this; if anything, consciousness of the subject is disrupting and confusing.

83 WASSILY KANDINSKY *Village Church* 1908

84 WASSILY KANDINSKY *Mountain Landscape with Church* 1910

There is an obvious parallel here to what the Brücke artists in Dresden were trying to do during the same period. The concentration on the impression made by nature, rather than on the physiognomy of nature itself, was intended in both cases to intensify expression. The characteristic common to both is elemental, archaic power. The artist's will is directed by his instinct, by the feeling an experience arouses in him, though in Kandinsky's case his consciousness retained more control.

The early paintings of Matisse had encouraged him as they had the Brücke. Kandinsky later acknowledged their common ground when he declared that he had moved to abstract painting from Expressionism.

This development took place 'by way of innumerable experiments, despair, hope, discoveries', not, at any event, in a straightforward progression, withdrawing from naturalism step by orderly step. Up to 1913 Kandinsky went on painting pictures on, or at least related to, specific subjects concurrently with his abstract paintings, although the latter gradually became more frequent. He explained this situation when he wrote:

> I have never been able to bring myself to use a form which came to me by some logical way, which had not arisen purely within my feelings. I was unable to invent forms, and the sight of such forms always disgusts me. All the forms I ever used came of their own accord, they presented themselves to me already shaped, and all I had to do was copy them, or else they took shape while I worked, often surprising me. With the years I have only learned how to exercise a certain degree of control over this imaginative power of mine. I have trained myself not simply to let myself go, but to put reins on the power that works within me, and to guide it.

85 From 1909 onwards Kandinsky was painting pictures like *Mountain*, which are considered non-figurative, although they contain ciphers of natural objects. The colours are purely expressive, completely detached from any associations. This position formed the salient from which Kandinsky made his first, initially isolated, sortie into complete abstraction in 1910. He himself had difficulties in experiencing purely abstract forms without the footing provided by an object. Moreover, since objects have a certain psychic resonance on their own account, abbreviated references to objects continuously crop up as 'psychic
86 chords', as in *Improvisation No. 19* of 1911, for instance, where they also help to create the third dimension. In 1912 Kandinsky progressed
98 to large compositions, like *With a Black Arc*. A systematic arrangement of planes, overlapping and interpenetrating each other, creates a picture space in which the colours thrust dramatically together.
99 *Dreamy Improvisation* of 1913 shows that this means was capable of expressing light-hearted gaiety as well as violent and serious moods.

Kandinsky was now in complete control of his means. The colours lie as if on a uniform surface, and it is only in the variation of the inner weight of the colours that different picture planes and spheres are evoked. The weights are so distributed that no architectonic centre is created. In this way Kandinsky avoided the ornamental. It was now possible to erase all the ciphers of natural objects from his pictures.

'Mystery speaking through mysteries. Isn't that meaning? Isn't that the conscious or unconscious purpose of the compulsive urge to create?' Kandinsky had asked in 1910. Now he knew the answer. He had reached the summit of what has been called Expressionist abstraction.

85 WASSILY KANDINSKY
Mountain 1909

86 WASSILY KANDINSKY
Improvisation on No. 19
1911

Alexey Yavlensky (whose name is more familiar in its German trans-literation) had come to Munich in 1896, as had Kandinsky; like him, he had entered Anton Azbe's school. He was the better prepared and equipped of the two. He started to paint in Moscow in 1884, as a twenty-year-old lieutenant. In 1889 he got himself transferred to St Petersburg and was able to attend the academy there. It was not long before he entered the circle of Ilya Repin, the most distinguished Russian painter of the day, and met Marianne Werefkin.

Even in the early pictures dating from the first years of the new century, it is evident that colour was his natural medium of expression. The constant factors that run right through the whole of Jawlensky's output are already apparent. Colour is not there to serve the representa-tion of an object, of something material, but the object serves as the starting-point for the arrangement of colours. His fundamental characteristics of mysticism and of remoteness from illustration are also present. From the first he restricted his subject-fields to still-life, landscape and the human figure, which he eventually reduced to the face alone.

The sequence of experiences that Jawlensky looked for was similar to Kandinsky's. But Kandinsky, the more discriminating and complex of the two, stored the experiences and influences that he encountered within himself, and then released them all at once. Jawlensky, on the contrary, tried to assimilate and react to each influence immediately, which brought Kandinsky's unwarranted derision down upon his head. 'Frankly, I think there's something wrong with Jawlensky's dots. Anybody can pick up that style if they want to.'

In the same year, 1903, Jawlensky went to Normandy and Paris. He was profoundly influenced by Van Gogh, whose influence manifested itself in him, as in so many other artists, in a crude kind of Pointillism. In 1905 Jawlensky went to Brittany. 'Here I did a great deal of work. And I understood how to transfer nature into colours appropriate to the ardour of my soul. I painted a large number of landscapes there, bushes and Breton heads from my window. The pictures were glow-ing with colour. And my inner self was contented.'

At that stage Jawlensky was assimilating the practice and aesthetic theory of the Pont-Aven School. He was able to show ten of his Breton paintings at the 1905 Salon d'Automne, the exhibition which gave birth to the term 'Fauves'.

87 ALEXEJ VON
JAWLENSKY *Yellow
Houses* 1909

This exhibition and a meeting with Matisse gave Jawlensky unmistakable reassurance in what he was trying to do. He wrote in 1905:

My friends, the apples that I love for their delightful red, yellow, mauve
and green clothing cease to be apples for me when I see them against this
or that background, in such or such surroundings. Their tones and their
radiant colours dissolve, on the basis of other, sober tones, into a harmony
threaded with dissonances. And they resound in my sight like a music
reproducing this or that mood of my soul, this or that fleeting contact
with the soul of things, with that Something, unsuspected and ignored
by all, which trembles in every object of the material world, in every
impression that we receive from outside ourselves. To reproduce the
things which exist without being, to reveal them to other people, by
passing them through my sympathetic understanding, by revealing them
in the passion I feel for them, that is the goal of my artistic existence. To
me, apples, trees, human faces are no more than hints as to what else I
should see in them: the life of colour, comprehended by a passionate
lover.

In 1907 he went to Paris again to work in Matisse's studio. Armed in this way, Jawlensky was able to make a valuable contribution to the communal work of the group of friends in 1908. He, too, benefited from their summer together, acquiring a breadth in his landscapes 87 (*Yellow Houses*) which brings to the fore the static quality, the severity of their composition. The contours are drawn in darkly to hold the brilliant masses of colour on the surface plane. There are no human figures in the landscapes, so that they avoid narrative. They are without anecdote or spatial dimension, as are his still-lifes, such as *Still-life* 88 *with Fruit* of 1910, which used to belong to Kandinsky.

Still-life or landscape, the motifs are interchangeable. Increasingly, too, they become less and less susceptible to definition. The landscape 89 entitled *Solitude* of 1912 shows this. The contouring is less prominent than before, being replaced by bands of colour which have an intensifying effect on each other and serve to give the motif even more symbolic significance. That is the 'synthesis' which Jawlensky had

88 ALEXEJ VON JAWLENSKY *Still-life with Fruit c.* 1910

89 ALEXEJ VON JAWLENSKY *Solitude* 1912

always preached, and which had become the programme of the
Neue Künstlervereinigung: the use of artistic forms to express the
interpenetration of impressions of the external world and experiences
of the inner world.

The portraits of 1909, such as *Girl with Peonies*, are Jawlensky's   97
most beautiful and probably most popular works. These paintings are
still portraits in the conventional sense. But even in his treatment of the
human figure Jawlensky was quickly moving towards simplification.
His representation of the subject concentrated more and more on the
head, in which the eyes became the dominant formal element. Form
became increasingly monumental and ideographic. The pictures bear
general titles like *Russian Girl*, *Woman with Green Fan* or *Spanish Girl
with Black Shawl*. Jawlensky's personal style was fully developed from   90
1911. He spent the summer at Prerow on the Baltic coast, where

Heckel was painting in the same year, before going to Paris for the last time to meet Matisse and Van Dongen.

> This summer marked a great development in my art. I painted the best landscapes of my career to date while I was there, and large figural works in strong, glowing colours, absolutely not naturalistic or material-ish. I used a great deal of red, blue, orange, cadmium yellow, chrome-oxide green. The forms were very emphatically contoured in Prussian blue, and emerged irresistibly from an inner ecstasy.

He was therefore no longer able to find any kinship of intention or of feeling in Paris, but discovered them instead in Nolde, whom he met in 1912. 'His pictures remind me of my own in the strength of their expression. I have a passionate love for Nolde and his art', Jawlensky confessed. The outbreak of war in 1914 had a significance for the Russian over and above the need to leave Germany and seek refuge at Saint-Prex on Lake Geneva. The psychological shock put an end to his development of 'sensuous painting'. Expression had to give way to contemplation. 'I understood that I must not paint what I saw, nor even what I felt, but only what lived within me, in my soul . . . the world of nature that lay before me was no more than the prompter.'

90 ALEXEJ VON JAWLENSKY
Spanish Girl with Black Shawl
1913

91 ALEXEJ VON JAWLENSKY
Large Female Head
1917

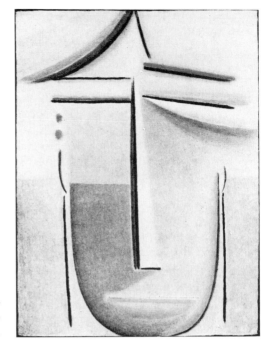

92 ALEXEJ VON JAWLENSKY
Divine Radiance
1918

Jawlensky's meditations took fruit in a series of small *Variations on a Landscape Theme*, most of which were painted between 1914 and 1918. In 1915 he turned once more to the depiction of the human face. In innumerable variations he pushed the theme further and further beyond the bounds of the individual, and in the process came remarkably close in some respects to Schmidt-Rottluff's style, as in *Large Female Head* 91 of 1917. The further the remove from realism, the more apparent his religious fervour became. Reduced to a simple geometrical structure, the human face expanded to become a devotional picture, for 'art is the longing for God'.

GABRIELE MÜNTER

In his introduction to the catalogue of an exhibition shown in Munich in 1913, which included works by Gabriele Münter, Kandinsky wrote:

> We can only assert here, with especial satisfaction, that Gabriele Münter's talent, robust, rooted in an inward strength and sensitivity, in fact genuinely German, should in no circumstances be assessed as masculine, or as 'quasi-masculine'. This talent – and we emphasize it, once more, with great satisfaction – can only be described as exclusively and purely

feminine. . . . It gives us especial pleasure to realize that it is impossible to explain the source of this particular conviction. Gabriele Münter does not paint 'feminine' subjects, she does not work with feminine materials, and does not permit herself any feminine coquetry. There are neither raptures, nor agreeable exterior elegance, nor appealing weaknesses to be found here. Nor, on the other hand, are there any masculine charms either: no 'sinewy brushwork', no heaps of paint 'hurled on to the canvas'. The pictures are painted throughout with a delicately and correctly sensed measure of external strength, with not a trace of feminine or masculine coquetry in the 'making'. We could almost say that they are painted modestly, i.e. that they were inspired, not by a desire for outward display, but by a purely inward compulsion.

Kandinsky first met Gabriele Münter in 1902, when she was twenty-five and came to him as a pupil in the Phalanx School. She had already studied under various teachers in Düsseldorf and Munich. She possessed natural talent but lacked ambition, so that her life and her work already followed a path that could be described as 'unconscious, uncalculated, without plan, unconsidered, perhaps rather dreamy'. She poured out her gifts without reflection or concern. She constantly

doubted the necessity and importance of her art and of art in general. Her lessons with Kandinsky made an impression on her. 'That was a new artistic experience; Kandinsky was quite unlike the other teachers, and explained things thoroughly and penetratingly and regarded me as a human being with conscious aspirations, capable of setting myself targets to aim for. It was new to me and impressed me.' Kandinsky, too, was so strongly impressed by her personality both as woman and as artist that he became engaged to her in 1903, although he was still married. They lived together until Kandinsky's return to Russia in 1916.

It was her unquestioning naivety that gave Gabriele Münter the confidence necessary to prevent her becoming dependent on Kandinsky, but enabled her to remain a counterpoise to his complexity, his intellectualized pursuit of conscious goals. Her Impressionistic pictures of 1906–07, painted with the palette-knife, do indeed have considerable similarities to Kandinsky's work of the same period, but the decisive artistic influence on her was Jawlensky. The Fauve works she had seen in Paris with Kandinsky, and her own large-format woodcuts (*Kandinsky*, 1906), of which she showed twenty-four in *94*

93 GABRIELE MÜNTER
View of Murnau Moss
1908

94 GABRIELE MÜNTER
Kandinsky 1906

95 WASSILY KANDINSKY *Landscape with Tower* 1909

96 GABRIELE MÜNTER *Still-life with St George* 1911

97 ALEXEJ VON JAWLENSKY *Girl with Peonies* 1909

Bonn in 1908, had prepared her for the decisive stimulus which she, too, found in Murnau in 1908. She discovered for herself the Bavarian folk-art of painting behind glass, being perhaps the first of the Blauer Reiter circle to do so, and at the same time was able to observe in Jawlensky's work the juxtaposition of brilliant, strongly contoured planes of colour, which also became a characteristic of her own work
93 (*View of Murnau Moss*, 1908). She wrote of the months in Murnau, in her diary for 1911: 'After a short period of torment I made a great leap forward, from painting straight from nature – more or less impressionistically – to sensing a meaning – to abstracting – to giving an extract. It was a glorious time of interesting, joyful work, with many conversations about art.'

Gabriele Münter's favourite subject, after landscape, was still-life.
96 A picture like *Still-life with St George*, which was reproduced in *Der Blaue Reiter*, shows very clearly the character of her personal style. Kandinsky summarized it in these terms:

> She has the following characteristics: (1) An accurate, discreet, delicate and yet well-defined style of drawing, which is composed of the elements of mischief, melancholy and reverie, truly German characteristics . . . to be seen in the old German masters, and to be heard in German folk music and folk verse. (2) A simple harmonic system of her own, consisting of a certain range of none but serious colours, which, by reason of its deep tones, composes a serene chord with her drawing. This kind of colour-harmony is to be seen in old German paintings on glass, paintings behind glass, and in the work of the German Primitives, such as the Master of the Life of Mary.

Instinctively and spontaneously, unhampered by stylistic preconceptions, Gabriele Münter succeeded in formulating solutions which assured her of a place in the Blauer Reiter circle on her own merits. She had a significance over and above the fact of being Kandinsky's inseparable companion for thirteen years, although the eventual separation did put an almost complete halt to her work for a very long time. She later admitted:

> If I modelled myself on any artist, and that was the case to a certain extent between 1903 and 1913, then it was probably on Van Gogh, as transmitted to me by Jawlensky and his theories (his talk of synthesis). But that cannot be compared to what Kandinsky meant to me. He loved and understood my talent, protected it and fostered it.

The second exhibition of the Neue Künstlervereinigung, in September 1910, confirmed Franz Marc in his own efforts at a turning-point in his development. Without yet being a member of the alliance, he went to its defence against the general chorus of condemnation:

> All the pictures include a plus-factor, which robs the public of its pleasure, but which is in every case the principal merit of the work: the completely spiritualized, de-materialized inwardness of perception which our fathers, the artists of the nineteenth century, never even tried to achieve in their 'pictures'. This bold undertaking, to take the *matière* which Impressionism sank its teeth into, and spiritualize it, is a necessary reaction, which began with Gauguin in Pont-Aven and has already fostered innumerable experiments. . . . The way the Munich public condemns the exhibition is almost amusing. They behave as if the paintings were a few isolated aberrations of sick minds, whereas in fact they are the sober, austere beginnings on soil that is being turned for the first time. Don't they know that the same innovatory creative spirit, resolute and confident, is active in every corner of Europe today?

These exemplars were of the greatest value to Marc. He knew that Kandinsky and his circle were his allies, sharing the aim of his artistic endeavour, to assert the spiritual in art. Marc had written to the publisher Reinhard Piper in 1908: 'I am trying to intensify my ability to sense the organic rhythm that beats in all things, to develop a pantheistic sympathy for the trembling and flow of blood in nature, in trees, in animals, in the air – I am trying to make a picture from it, with new movements and with colours which make a mockery of the old kind of studio picture.'

Religion, for Marc, was an important component of art. He took heart from museums where people could learn everything, 'namely the one great truth, that there is no great, pure art without religion, that the more religious art has been, the more artistic it has been.'

And in the almanac *Der Blaue Reiter*, he formulated the goal that young artists should seek: 'To create in their work symbols for their age, which will go on the altars of the coming spiritual religion.'

Franz Marc had at first thought of studying theology, then enrolled at Munich University as a student of languages, and suddenly decided to be a painter. He attended the academy in Munich until 1903, when he went to Paris for the first time. The encounter with the works of the Impressionists was a turning-point in his life, according to his diary, but there is no visible trace of it in his paintings. Again on his second visit to Paris in 1907, he walked among Impressionist paintings 'like a roe-deer in an enchanted forest, for which it has always yearned'. But the only lasting impression he received was from Van Gogh. On his return he noted: 'Art is nothing but the expression of our dream; the more we surrender to it the closer we get to the inner truth of things, our dream-life, the true life that scorns questions and does not see them.'

That was certainly the opposite of what Impressionism aimed at, but Marc did not possess the means to express his perceptions. In order to get closer to 'the inner truth of things', he spent the following years trying to develop his imaginative faculties by 'learning nature by heart'. 'I make the most outrageous demands on my imagination and

98 WASSILY KANDINSKY *With a Black Arc* 1912

99 WASSILY KANDINSKY *Dreamy Improvisation* 1913

leave aside everything else, theory and nature study, as other people understand them. This is the only way I can work, drawing on nothing but my own faculty of imagination, which I feed without stint – except in working hours', he wrote to Macke in 1910.

He made an intensive study of animal anatomy, in order to arrive at a system of rules of form. He even gave lessons in anatomy up to 1910, to earn money. His aim was to have such a mastery of anatomy as to be able, within reason, to invent new beings, which would still be natural in their effect, because they would be constructed in accordance with the rules of nature. These were the prerequisites for being able to paint the most simple of things, 'for that alone contains the symbolism, the pathos and the mystery of nature'. But up till 1910

127

he was unable to master the 'randomness' of nature in chromatic terms, so that the most successful expression of his aims is the little sculpture *Panther* of 1908. His large paintings, on the other hand, he destroyed year after year, because they did not measure up to his requirements.

100 Marc also made a close study of the nude up to 1912 (*Nude with Cat*, 1910), but he was unable to produce anything that completely satisfied him. He could not create as complete a sympathy between his human models and the rhythm of nature as he could with animals. 'The impious people that surrounded me (especially the men) did not stir my real feelings, while the untouched instinct of animals for life struck a chord of all that is best in me', Marc wrote to his wife in 1915.

The year 1910 was an eventful one for Marc, and helped him decisively forward on his road towards a satisfactory realization of his artistic vision. In the spring he held his first exhibition, in the gallery of the Munich dealer Brackl, showing pictures whose basic tonal pattern was still very light, permeated with a sense of the open air. Since their treatment of the subject was still realistic, the critics' reaction was extremely favourable, and Marc was hailed as a promising young talent.

He got to know August Macke at the same period, and through him the collector Bernard Koehler. Soon Koehler was paying Marc a monthly allowance which relieved him of the most pressing cares of everyday existence.

It was Macke who deliberately drew Marc's attention to the independent expressive power of colour. Macke made him even more conscious of the dichotomy between the large-scale conception and abstract tendency of his forms and the naturalism of his colouring. He wrote to Macke in November 1910: 'The harvest of your summer is displayed on our walls. I like some of them terrifically. The "certainty" with which most of it is done often makes me feel ashamed of myself. The thousand steps that I need to take for a picture are of no advantage, as I sometimes foolishly used to think. Things must change.'

He was now seeking the rules governing colour with the same intensity that he had pursued the mastery of form in the past. He wrote to Macke in December:

> You know my tendency is always to imagine things in my head and to work from this idea. I am going to explain my theory of blue, yellow and red, which will probably seem as 'Spanish' to you as my face.
> Blue is the male principle, astringent and spiritual.

100 FRANZ MARC
Nude with Cat 1910

Yellow the female principle, gentle, gay and sensual.

Red is matter, brutal and heavy and always the colour to be opposed and overcome by the other two!

For example, if you mix serious, spiritual blue with red, you intensify the blue to unbearable sorrow, and yellow the conciliatory, the complementary colour to purple, becomes indispensable.

(Woman as consoler, not as lover!)

If you mix red and yellow to make orange, you turn passive, feminine yellow into a Fury, with a sensual force that again makes cool, spiritual blue indispensable, the man, and in fact blue always places itself at once and automatically at the side of orange, the colours love each other. Blue and orange, a thoroughly festive sound.

But then if you mix blue and yellow to make green, you arouse red, matter, the 'earth', but here, as a painter, I always sense a difference: it is never possible altogether to subdue eternally material, brutal red with green alone, as with the other colour chords. (Just think of some handicraft objects in red and green!) Green always needs the help of some more blue (sky) and yellow (sun) in order to silence matter.

101 FRANZ MARC
The Red Horses 1911

102 FRANZ MARC
Blue Horse I 1911

103 FRANZ MARC *Red Roe Deer II* 1912

The contact with friends in the Neue Künstlervereinigung who were further advanced along the same road as himself, helped Marc to progress rapidly. He pondered for a long time over Werefkin's remark that nearly all the Germans had made the error of mistaking light for colour, whereas colour is something quite different which has absolutely nothing to do with light, i.e. illumination. He tried to make colour purely a channel of expression, and wrote to his wife in February 1911:

> Am working very hard and struggling to get a grip of form and expression. There are no 'subjects' and no 'colours' in art, only expression! In conventional usage, the words 'colourist' and 'colouristic' are nonsense. I already knew before that expression is what matters in the last analysis. But when I set to work I found other things that seemed to 'matter': 'the probabilities', for instance, the pleasing sound of colours, so-called 'harmony' etc. . . . But we ought not to bother about anything but the expression in a picture. A picture is a cosmos which is subject to a quite different set of laws from nature. Nature is lawless, infinite, an endless

spread of elements without order. Our intellect makes its own narrow, rigid laws, so as to be able to reproduce infinite nature. The more severe the laws are, the more they cast aside the 'means' of nature, which have nothing to do with art. . . . Every art has begun its decline at the moment when it relinquished the severity of its laws, when it began to 'naturalize'. I write as if I had already seen the tablets of the laws of which I dream. But I am looking for them with all the longing of my soul and with all my strength, and my pictures already reveal a faint sense of them.

This was the spirit in which the animal pictures of 1911 were painted. With the *Red Horses* he finally reduced his subject-matter to the formulaic terms which had been his objective for years. Released from nature, colour is able to radiate its essence. 'I will never paint a bush blue for the sake of decorative effect, but only in order to intensify the whole reality of the horse to which it forms the background', he explained. Colour now balances the organic rhythm of form. From now on, whether Marc was painting *Large Blue Horses*, the *Monkey Frieze* or a single *Blue Horse*, his compositions needed no external justification. 'Every animal is the embodiment of his cosmic rhythm', as the poet Theodor Däubler wrote.

Marc had come close to reaching his goal, the 'animalization of art'. On the basis of his achievements, he was invited to join the Neue Künstlervereinigung. He soon became the group's most eloquent agitator, beside Kandinsky. It was he who made possible the publication of *Der Blaue Reiter*, who persuaded the publisher Reinhard Piper to bring out Kandinsky's *Über das Geistige in der Kunst* ('On the Spiritual in Art'), and who seized every opportunity of expounding and explaining to the wider public. He wrote, for instance, in the magazine *Pan* in 1912:

Do people seriously believe that we new artists do not take our form from nature, do not wrest it from nature, just like every artist that has ever lived? . . . Nature glows in our paintings as it does in all art. . . . Nature is everywhere, in us and outside us; but there is something which is not quite nature but rather the mastery and interpretation of nature: art. In its essence, art has always been the boldest removal from nature and 'naturalness'. The bridge across to the realm of the spirit, the necromancy of humanity.

The same article includes the sentence: 'We no longer cling to reproduction of nature, but destroy it, so as to reveal the mighty laws which hold sway behind the beautiful exterior.' That is what Marc

104 FRANZ MARC *Tiger* 1912

was trying to do in bringing the individual forms of animals and landscape closer to each other in a single flow of rhythm. Sometimes he did
it with soft, fluid lines, as in the picture *Red Roe Deer II* of 1912, which   *103*
resulted, however, in a noticeable loss of tension in the composition,
and at other times with forms reduced to angular cubes, as in the *Tiger*,   *104*
also of 1912. But while the individual form is 'Cubist', the picture as a
whole is not. This interpenetration of subject and surroundings was
what Marc meant when he wrote of the 'mystic-inward construction'
of a Cubist painting by Picasso, in *Der Blaue Reiter*. He also found
something of the sort in the Futurists, in the reproduction of actual
movement by the rhythmicization of the picture's elements.

133

105 FRANZ MARC *The Mandrill* 1913

106 FRANZ MARC *Animal Fates* 1913

107 FRANZ MARC *Tyrol* 1913–14

In the autumn of 1912 Marc and Macke went to Paris and visited Delaunay, who had taken part in the two Blauer Reiter exhibitions. They saw Delaunay's window-pictures, which made a great impression on Marc. He adopted their transparency and crystalline play of forms. The pictures of 1913, such as *Deer in the Forest II*, *Mandrill* and *Animal Fates*, all depict the interpenetration of animal and landscape in the dissection, overlapping and interlocking of forms that have become transparent. The mystic significance emerges in the completely unified rhythm of the picture plane.

105
106

108 FRANZ MARC *Struggling Forms* 1914

When Herwarth Walden mounted the Erster Deutscher Herbstsalon in Berlin in 1913, Marc played an important role in the selection and hanging, and was struck by the extent to which the artists represented were using abstract forms. He soon abandoned the subject altogether, and occupied himself in 1914 almost entirely with abstract composi-
108 tions, to which he gave titles like *Struggling Forms, Cheerful Forms, Playing Forms* or *Broken Forms.* He wrote in explanation:

> I felt the human form to be ugly from a very early stage, animals seemed to be more beautiful, purer; but in them, too, I came to discover so much that was repulsive and ugly that my depiction of them instinctively, on an inner compulsion, became increasingly more schematic, more abstract. Trees, flowers, the earth, everything revealed more ugly and repulsive sides to me every year, until now at last I have become fully conscious of the ugliness of nature, its impurity.

And yet it looks as though the abstract paintings, too, were another transitional stage in his development. The last painting on his easel

136

was *Tyrol*, which he painted in 1913 and revised in 1914. It was a *107* mountain landscape conceived on an expansive scale, in which he depicted the struggle of light. In its final form he added a Madonna, as if in order to provide an interpretation of all his work in his last picture. Marc was killed at Verdun on 4 March 1916.

AUGUST MACKE

Macke was only twenty-three years old when he saw some drawings and lithographs by Franz Marc in the gallery of the Munich dealer Brackl early in 1910, which inspired him at once to seek the artist out. The deep and unshakeable friendship which developed between the two artists did not, however, mislead Macke into making common cause with the older man's aspirations. In the summer of 1910 Marc tried to found an artists' association, and dreamt of a periodical with the title *Blaue Blätter*; so it was a natural step for him to join the Neue Künstlervereinigung. Macke, on the other hand, always maintained greater reserve. He wrote to Marc in September 1910: 'I have been in Munich this week, and got to know the whole Neue Künstler-vereinigung at Thannhauser's – Jawlensky, Kandinsky, etc. For Munich they are very, very good. I was interested.' On 26 December he added:

> I have been to Hagen, saw two Matisses, which enchanted me. A large collection of Japanese masks. Sublime! Neue Vereinigung were hung in a bad light. . . . Kandinsky, Jawlensky, Bechtejeff and Erbslöh have immense artistic sensibility. But the means of expression are too big for what they have to say. The sound of their voice is so good, so fine, that what is being said gets lost. Consequently a human element is missing. They concentrate too much, I think, on form. There is much to be learnt from their efforts. But early things by Kandinsky, and a few by Jawlensky too, seem a little empty to me. And Jawlensky's heads looked at me a little bit too much with colours. With blue and green. I hope you understand what I mean. To me they fail to be great because they lack the self-evident quality that is in Busch and Daumier, and sometimes in Matisse or Japanese erotica.

Macke's reservations were not diminished by his involvement in *Der Blaue Reiter*, to which he contributed an article on masks, or by his participation, from Bonn, in the Blauer Reiter exhibitions.

In fact Macke painted only one symbolic-abstract painting, which expressed directly the impression that Marc and Kandinsky made.

Significantly the two editors chose to reproduce this picture, *Storm*, which was painted in October 1911 while they were all working on the almanac, both in the catalogue of the first Blauer Reiter exhibition and in the almanac itself. Macke himself had already moved on beyond this stage by the spring of 1912, just as there were a lot of other things that he had taken up for a time and then abandoned again.

From 1904 to 1906 he had attended art school in Düsseldorf and designed costumes and sets for the theatre there. He discovered Impressionism in Julius Meier-Graefe's book *Manet und sein Kreis* ('Manet and his Circle'), and went to Paris in the summer of 1907. Manet made the strongest impression on him, then Degas, whose pastels struck him as more original than anything he had ever seen. His Paris experiences awoke a compulsion in him. He experimented with pure colours and seized every opportunity of adding to his knowledge and skill. In the autumn of 1907 he went to Berlin to spend six months as the pupil of Corinth. In the summer of 1908 he returned to Paris, where he was most struck by Cézanne, Seurat and Gauguin. He went

109 AUGUST MACKE *Girls among Trees* 1914

110 AUGUST MACKE *Lady in a Green Jacket* 1913

to Paris again in 1909, this time in the company of Louis Moilliet.
Immediately after this he went to the Tegernsee, a lake in northern
Bavaria, on the invitation of a friend, the writer Wilhelm Schmidt-
bonn; he spent a year there, during which, on a visit to Munich, he
discovered Marc.

139

111 AUGUST MACKE *Zoological Garden I* 1912

There is a description of the Macke of this period in the diary, for 1908, of his friend Lothar Erdmann:

Everything he paints is a search, a self-development, a striving for under-standing of the most profound kind. He is still experimenting, not executing, he often paints two, three pictures in a day, and his sketchbooks are already innumerable. He lives in a continuous, sharp criticism of his work and is thus constantly changing and developing. His talent as a painter is by no means his only gift, his literary taste is of the highest, clear and assured, and he is interested to a certain extent in philosophy and science. Musically he is extraordinarily receptive, his psychology is penetrating, often one-sided but always shrewd, so that there is hardly anyone that I would rather discuss people with. He has, by nature, absolutely no interest in the transcendental. His sensibility is elemental and deep. He experiences – I would say – those many moments of ecstasy, the alternation between the greatest happiness and the deepest depression, which are the lot of a great artist, who must learn the whole gamut of feeling from his own experience. His genius is great enough for him to be able to mock and caricature sublime things without diminishing their importance for him. . . . He has an insatiable curiosity for life and

112 AUGUST MACKE *Large, Well-lit Shop Window* 1912

113 AUGUST MACKE *Kairouan I* 1914

has the ability to satisfy it. In addition he has the sort of good luck reserved for the darlings of the gods.

The year beside the Tegernsee produced about two hundred pictures. It was while he was there that Macke came to recognize the true goal of his work. He wrote in a letter: 'I'm working fearfully hard now. Working, for me, means celebrating everything simultaneously, nature, sunlight and trees, plants, people, animals, flowers and pots, tables, chairs, mountains, the reflection of water on growing things.' In this frame of mind a Matisse exhibition in Munich was a tremendous experience for him, and his enthusiasm for Matisse was still pouring forth in letters to Marc at the end of 1910. He was now at last

114 PAUL KLEE *The Föhn Wind in the Marcs' Garden* 1915

1915 102

able to evaluate in structural terms something of what he had experienced in 1907 when he had been preoccupied with pure colour. But it remained characteristic of Macke that he always took the subject as his starting-point and did not allow the artistic problems to impinge until he was actually at work on the picture. That is what gave him the 'certainty' by which Marc felt himself put to shame.

Macke's encounter with the Blauer Reiter, and his rejection of the group's dramatization of the content of art, led him to clarify his idea of what painting meant for him, namely giving an artistic form to impressions of the visible, material world. Cubism showed him the way. He had seen the works of Picasso, Le Fauconnier, and above all Delaunay, at the exhibitions of the Neue Künstlervereinigung and Blauer Reiter and at Alfred Flechtheim's gallery in Düsseldorf. A letter he wrote about the Sonderbund exhibition contains the significant cry, 'Picasso! Picasso! Picasso!' Macke himself showed *Walkers Beside the Sea* at this exhibition, which is composed predominantly of angular forms with sharp corners. The formal unity he imposed on landscape, people and animals was not, in his case, the outcome of his pondering of theoretical problems, but reflected his experience of reality. He was therefore never in any danger of stylistic imitation. *Zoological Garden I* of 1912, for instance, represents Macke's evaluation of all the experience he had accumulated to that date, dominated by his own unique kind of chromatic radiance.

111

An exhibition of Futurists in 1912 brought yet more new impressions. He experimented with the possibility of allowing impressions that were separated in time and space to merge into one another in a series of variations on the theme of a woman standing before a shop window (*Large, Well-lit Shop Window*, 1912). Once again, the theory hardly interested him at all. In March 1913 he wrote to the philosopher Eberhard Grisebach:

112

Cubism, Futurism, Expressionism, abstract painting, are only names given to a change which our artistic thinking wants to make and is making. Nobody has ever painted falling raindrops suspended in the air, they've always been depicted as streaks (even the cave-men drew herds of reindeer in the same way). Now people are painting cabs rattling along, lights flickering, people dancing, all in the same way (this is how we all see movement). That is the whole frightfully simple secret of Futurism. It's very easy to prove its artistic feasibility, for all the philosophizing that has been raised against it. Space, surface and time are different things, which ought not to be mixed together, is the continuous cry. If only it were possible to separate them. I can't do it. Time has a large part to play in looking at a picture. A picture (a stupid empty surface to begin with) gets covered, in the course of its creation, by a rhythmically measured network of colours, lines and dots, which evokes in its final form a total of living movement. The eye jumps from a blue to red, to green (even if there is only a change of form), to a black line, suddenly comes upon a sharp white eruption, follows it, floats on to a delicate yellow patch, from which little red patches are released, the little red patches turn green and all at once the eye runs over the blue, red and green again, led on by different forms this time, starting on a new cycle. Whole sections appear as warm, orange, vermilion, others cold, black, blue, white, grey. It is impossible to take it all in at once. Time is inseparable from surface.

A trip to Paris with Marc in the autumn of 1912 was even more important for Macke. A call paid on Delaunay led quickly to the establishment of a close relationship. They wrote to each other, and Delaunay and Apollinaire visited Macke in Bonn in February 1913. The spatial values of colour that Delaunay demonstrated, and his *contraste simultané*, the harmony of colours that separate and unite simultaneously, moved Macke deeply. 'He gives movement itself,' Macke wrote; 'the Futurists illustrate movement.' Armed with perceptions like these, Macke went to Lake Thun in Switzerland in autumn, 1913. In the eight months he spent there Macke saw the whole beauty of the world, and translated it in his art into a magical feast of colour, 'world as visual poetry'. This was the period when he painted pictures such as *Promenade*, *Lady in a Green Jacket* and *Girls Bathing*.

110, 1

He remained uncommitted to any one style, painting in both a softer, flowing style and in a more austere, geometric one in the same period. He wrote to the artist Hans Thuar:

> The new discovery that I have made in painting is the following. There are chords of colours, let's say a certain red and green, which move, shimmer when you look at them. Now, if you're looking at a tree in a landscape, you can either look at the tree, or at the landscape, but not both because of the stereoscopic effect. Now when you're painting something three-dimensional, the chromatic sound which shimmers is the three-dimensional effect of colour, and when you paint a landscape, and the green foliage shimmers a little with the blue sky showing through it, that happens because the green is on a different plane from the sky in nature too. Finding the space-shaping energies of colour, instead of contenting ourselves with a dead chiaroscuro, is our finest task.

145

115 AUGUST MACKE *Promenade* 1913

While beside Lake Thun, Macke conceived the idea of going to Tunis with Klee and Moilliet. Their famous trip in April 1914 lasted only two weeks. Macke brought back thirty-seven watercolours and hundreds of drawings. These are treasures, leaping spontaneously out
113   of the moment of their conception (*Kairouan I*), which illustrate the absolute mastery Macke had acquired by the age of twenty-seven. He had little time in which to make use of the wealth of new material
116   (*Turkish Café II*). When he got back to Bonn in June he had six weeks left, during which he took up earlier themes in a series of large paintings.
109   The one on his easel at the end was *Girls among Trees*. It imparts a sense of liberation, with all the gaiety and love of life that were Macke's birthright.

Macke was called up for military service on 8 August 1914; he was killed in Champagne on 26 September.

146

Paul Klee became friendly with Kandinsky in the autumn of 1911 and was drawn into the Blauer Reiter circle, but his approach was cautious and hesitant. Klee had been settled in Munich since 1906, and had first arrived there to study painting as early as 1898. He established contact with the progressive forces in art in Munich at an astonishingly late date. Exhibitions in Munich and journeys, such as the ones he made to Italy in 1901 with Hermann Haller (who later exhibited with the Neue Künstlervereinigung), and to Paris in 1905 with Moilliet (who was also a close friend of Macke's) had helped him to accumulate a store of experience similar to those of the artists who were later to be his friends. The major discoveries for him were Ensor, Munch, Cézanne and Van Gogh. In 1908, for instance, he wrote in his diary, *à propos* of two Van Gogh exhibitions:

> His emotion is alien to me, especially in my present phase, but he is quite certainly a genius. Pathologically emotional, he is a man always in peril, and capable of endangering those who do not look beyond him. A mind suffers here at the burning of a star. It is liberated in the work shortly before his catastrophe. The profoundest tragedy is enacted here, true tragedy, a tragedy of nature, an archetypal tragedy. I must be allowed my feelings of terror!

What he saw was not reflected directly in his own work, but helped him to define his own position. 'He who cannot do otherwise, i.e. who cannot do something else, finds his style. The way to style: Know thyself.' Klee soon came to understand what was the essence of the problem, the achievement of harmony between the inner and the external. He wrote of his progress towards this goal in his diary:

> The change of course was very abrupt; in the summer of 1908 I devoted myself entirely to natural phenomena and based the black-and-white landscapes behind glass of 1907–08 on these studies. Hardly have I reached this stage, when nature is boring me again. Perspectives make me yawn. Am I to distort them now? (I have already tried distortion in a mechanical way.) What other way is there for me to bridge the gap between inner and outer as freely as possible?

Ensor and Van Gogh showed him the potentiality of line as an independent structural element, capable of formulating a particular condition. Klee wrote late in 1908:

148

Given new strength by my naturalistic studies, I may now dare to tread once more my original ground of psychic improvisation. With the link to an impression of nature now only quite indirect, I may dare once more to give shape to what is actually weighing on my soul. To note down experiences, which could translate themselves into lines in complete darkness. This is a potentiality for original creation which has long existed, interrupted only temporarily by the timidity caused by isolation. In this way my essential personality will be able to speak, to free itself in the greatest freedom.

Klee achieved this goal in his drawings from 1909 onwards. With delicate, extraordinarily nervous, sensitive strokes, of which only a minority serve the delineation of objects, he produces a pure representation of the linear element, as in *Scene in Restaurant* of 1911.   *117*
Feelings, moods and the experiences of dreams resonate together in a single image which had grown purely from the imagination.

It was more difficult for Klee to combine drawing and colour, to transfer his 'basic ability' in drawing into his painting without losing it. He saw paintings by Cézanne in the Munich Secession in 1909. And although he noted: 'He is my teacher *par excellence*, much more so than Van Gogh', he was unable to draw the proper conclusion for a long time. At this period all the encouragement he received related to his drawing. In 1910 a collective exhibition toured Switzerland,

117 PAUL KLEE *Scene in Restaurant* 1911

followed by another in the spring of 1911 at the Thannhauser gallery in Munich. In 1910 Alfred Kubin bought one of Klee's works, and personal acquaintance followed not long after. In 1911 he met Macke through Moilliet.

So as not to remain permanently isolated, outwardly at least, Klee joined Sema, a new artists' group in Munich, to which Kubin and Schiele also belonged, though he built no great hopes on the association. Once again it was Moilliet who made the introduction that led to the most important friendship, that with Kandinsky.

Klee took part in the second Blauer Reiter exhibition. The acquaintance with Kandinsky and Marc confirmed him in his aims of progressing 'from prototypes to archetypes', of apprehending 'art as a simile of creation'. Klee's attention was drawn to the problem of local colour, and he came to a conclusion which he recorded in his diary in 1910: 'Nature and the study of nature are less important than one's attitude to the contents of the paint box. Some day I must be able to improvise on the colour keyboard of adjacent pots of paint.'

The Blauer Reiter exhibition aroused in Klee a desire to pay another exploratory visit to Paris. He went there for two weeks in April 1912, and saw exhibitions of Rousseau, Picasso and Braque at Uhde's, Derain, Vlaminck and Picasso at Kahnweiler's, and Matisse at Bernheim jeune's. He visited Delaunay and Le Fauconnier in their studios. In particular the meeting with Delaunay, whose essay on light Klee translated for *Der Sturm*, drew his attention to the qualitative and quantitative rules governing colour, which from then on continued to preoccupy him. But Klee did not yet feel capable of summing up his experiences and the influences to which he had been exposed, and continued to feel his way forward with the greatest caution. He had no desire to reach a goal too quickly, 'for there is nothing more critical than arriving at a goal'.

The great revelation of colour as an independent form of expression, a medium that he could and must use himself, came in April 1914, on his visit to Tunisia with Macke and Moilliet. On the very first day there, he noted: 'The sun of a sombre power. The chromatic clearness on land promising. Macke senses it too. We both know that we shall work well here. . . . Matter and dream at the same time, and, as the third, totally integrated element, myself. It's going to be good.'

The unity of colour and form, the synthesis of architectural constructions and pictorial construction, happened effortlessly under

118 PAUL KLEE
*In the Houses of
Saint-Germain
(Tunis)* 1914

the Tunisian skies. Klee painted in watercolours 'with great trans-   *118*
formation and with complete fidelity to nature'. After ten days he
wrote: 'I'm stopping work now. There is such a profound and gentle
pressure on me, I can feel it and am therefore confident, without
needing to work. Colour has got me. I don't need to run after it. It's
got me for ever, I know it. That is the meaning of this happy hour:
colour and I are one. I am a painter.'

Klee was now in the position to construct his paintings from
chromatic volume, to remember Cézanne and Delaunay, their
modulation of colour producing a honeycomb structure, rhythmic
in appearance, poetic in invention (*The Föhn Wind in the Marcs'*   *114*
Garden).

Although Klee did not play a leading role in the Blauer Reiter, he
understood and approved the group's common aim, the search for a
means of expression for the world of inner experience. So he was
always prepared to take part in joint projects under the heading of
'Expressionism'. In a lecture he gave in 1924 Klee stated:

In their times, our antipodes of yesterday, the Impressionists, were perfectly right to concentrate on the seedlings, the undergrowth of everyday appearances. But our beating heart drove us downwards, deep into the primal soil. What has grown from this burrowing, call it what you will, dream, ideal, fantasy, is only to be taken completely seriously when it is entirely devoted, in combination with the appropriate media, to the act of artistic creation. When that happens, those curiosities become realities, the realities of art, which make life just a little more extensive than it normally seems. Because they not only reproduce things seen with a greater or lesser degree of temperament, but make visible what has been perceived in secret.

HEINRICH CAMPENDONK

Marc met Heinrich Campendonk in 1911 and invited him to join him at Sindelsdorf. Born in Krefeld in 1889, Campendonk had studied at the Kunstgewerbeschule there with Thorn-Prikker from 1905 to 1909, his original intention probably being to become a textile designer. In 1910 he shared a studio with Helmut Macke, August's cousin, until he moved to be near Marc. Marc felt particularly responsible for him and tried to help him in every way. Perhaps not least because Campendonk very quickly grew very close to him as an artist. It was said of Marc, by Klee: 'He possessed a feminine urge to try and share his wealth with everyone. The fact that not everyone followed his path made him worry about it.'

119 Campendonk, at any rate, followed Marc, as is clear even in a painting of 1911 like *Leaping Horse*, which was also reproduced in the almanac *Der Blaue Reiter*. Also in 1911, the dealer Alfred Flechtheim angered Marc when he wrote to him:

> Now Campendonk. I haven't yet written to him about what I think of his last three tempera pictures, and I don't want to, because I am anything but enchanted with them. While his earlier oil paintings illustrate a strong, independent temperament, I find that these three works have been too strongly influenced by the excessively strong wind that blows from you and Kandinsky, with the result that Campendonk has lost much of his originality.... Don't you think it would be better if Campendonk worked on his own again?

Campendonk did not share the ideas that governed the work of his friends, and soon found himself in a rather decorative, fairy-tale world, very close to that of folk-art. Human and animal figures are

119 HEINRICH CAMPENDONK
Leaping Horse 1911

120 HEINRICH CAMPENDONK
Girl Playing a Shawm 1914

stiff and motionless, arranged on top of each other rather than behind each othcr among decorative plants and trees (*Girl Playing a Shawm,* 1914). Even so, some of Campendonk's pictures have a beauty of their own, full of a fairy-tale lyricism.

120

ALFRED KUBIN

To give forceful expression to what is essential – as it was put in the original circular issued by the Neue Künstlervereinigung – was a formula which certainly applied to the work of Alfred Kubin. In 1906, when he was twenty-nine years old, he painted a series of extraordinarily non-figurative pictures, inspired by what he had seen through a microscope.

> I deliberately laid aside every reminiscence of the given organization of nature and used bundles of spores and bracts, fragments resembling

crystals or shells, scraps of flesh or skin, leaf ornaments and thousands of other things to form compositions that over and over again, even while I was working, astonished me and filled me with deep satisfaction, made me as happy, in fact, as the act of creation has seldom made me before or since.

Kubin showed seven of these works in tempera at the first exhibition of the Neue Künstlervereinigung.

In the spring of 1909 Kubin's novel *Die andere Seite* ('The Other Side') was published; it included some account of his work as an artist. The impression the book made at the time is illustrated by a letter he received from the poet Max Dauthendey:

> That this modern age has turned to chaos in your sight is a pleasure to see, to smell and to taste. The age of scientific exactitude, of statistics, of educational prisons and of the void of god, has been changed into a beneficial wilderness by your brilliant inspirations; and mysticism, the giant spider which was trampled to death, is climbing down from the walls on to the dissecting table to lie like an intangible shadow between the tweezers and the microscope.

This was the factor which Kubin had in common with the progressive forces in art, and which bound him to them. His connection with the Neue Künstlervereinigung, dating from 1909, probably came about through Kandinsky. He took part in the alliance's exhibitions, and later in the second Blauer Reiter exhibition and the Herbstsalon organized by *Der Sturm*. Two of his drawings were reproduced in *121, 122* *Der Blaue Reiter*.

121 ALFRED KUBIN Drawing from the *Almanach der Blaue Reiter* 1911

122 ALFRED KUBIN Drawing from the *Almanach der Blaue Reiter* 1911

In 1913 Marc thought up a new project, which was never to come to fruition because of the war. He wrote to Kubin: 'Would you like to illustrate part of the Bible? Large format, very lavish; other participants: Kandinsky, Klee, Heckel, Kokoschka and me.' Kubin took on the Book of Daniel, which appeared in 1918.

The formal differences between members of the group were of little importance and were little regarded, for they were not the criterion for what united them, which was the 'spiritual in art'. Kubin succeeded in sweeping every trace of pure narrative from ideas that had been formed in dreams and daydreams, and in raising them to formal visions; and, for that reason, what Herwarth Walden wrote in the preface to the catalogue of the Herbstsalon applies not least to him also:

Art is the gift of something new, not the reproduction of something already in existence. He who wants to enjoy a fine fruit must sacrifice its peel. Not even the most beautiful peel will disguise the staleness of the fruit inside. The painter paints what he sees with his innermost senses, the expression of his being, 'all that is transient is only an image' to him, he plays life, every impression of the external becomes an expression of the internal in his hands. He bears and is borne by his inner visions.

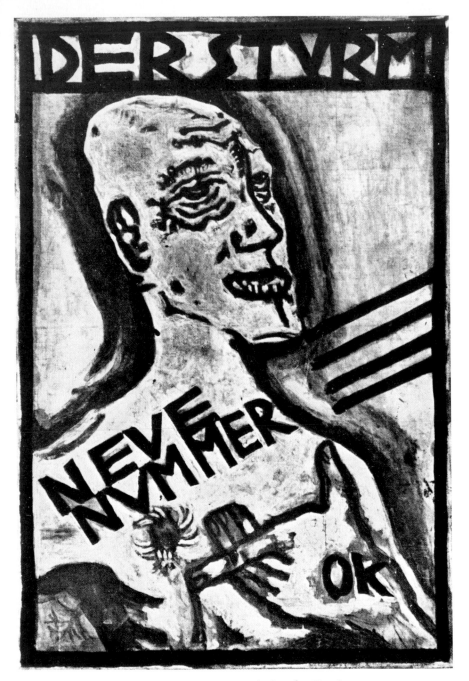

123 OSKAR KOKOSCHKA Poster design for *Der Sturm c.* 1910

CHAPTER FOUR

Berlin, Vienna, the Rhineland

DIE NEUE SEZESSION

In the autumn of 1911, when Marc wrote his article 'Die Wilden in Deutschland' ('The Fauves in Germany'), and named the Neue Sezession in Berlin as one of the centres of the movement, this group was making preparations for its fourth exhibition, in which artists from Prague and Munich (Neue Künstlervereinigung) were invited to take part as guests. The invitation offered the representatives of progressive art access to the most important platform in Germany. Since the turn of the century more and more artists had been drawn to the metropolis, whose rapid growth soon enabled it to offer economic opportunities that no other city in Germany could rival. The development was accelerated by the attempts made by the Berlin Secession, from its foundation in 1898, to attract artists from all over Germany to Berlin, in order to reinforce its own opposition to the official art encouraged by Kaiser Wilhelm II. The leaders of this opposition were the painter Max Liebermann and the dealer Paul Cassirer. In 1901 the Secession showed works by Van Gogh, and Paul Cassirer provoked the Kaiser's wrath with an exhibition of Cézanne. In 1902 Munch was represented at the Secession by seventy-two pictures, while Cassirer showed the first exhibition of Kubin. While these were on, the Siegesallee (Victory Avenue) was opened in Berlin, lined with thirty-two statues in Carrara marble. Wilhelm II, who had instigated the project, spoke of them enthusiastically in his speech, which included the following passage:

An art which presumes to overstep the limits and rules I have indicated is no longer art, it is an industry, it is a craft, and art must never be that. With that much misused word 'Freedom' and beneath its banner, people fall only too often into the total loss of all restraint and an excess of self-esteem. Anyone who departs from the law of beauty and the feeling for aesthetic harmony which every human being feels in his heart, even if he cannot express himself, anyone who attaches prime importance to one particular trend, one particular way of meeting purely technical demands, sins against the primal sources of art. But there is more: art should help to

157

educate a nation. It should give the lower classes the chance of raising themselves up, by way of the Ideal, after their hard toil and labour. The great ideals have become the heritage of us, the German nation, while other nations have lost them in greater or lesser degree. Only the German nation is left to follow the vocation of protecting, cherishing and propagating these great ideals, and one of these ideals is that we should give the working, the laborious classes the opportunity to raise themselves up to what is beautiful, and to work their way out of and above their other thoughts. But if art, as now happens all to often, does nothing more than present misery in an even more hideous form than it already possesses, then it sins against the German people.

Hermann Obrist made this reply in 1903:

Does a walk among the monuments in the Tiergarten in Berlin excite us like *Die Meistersinger von Nürnberg*? It does not . . . the whole empire is littered with monuments to soldiers and monuments to Kaiser Wilhelm of the same conventional type, which looks as if it were invented expressly to meet the taste of a fireman or someone like that. . . . We get the monuments we deserve. . . . Visual art should give images, not impressions; instead of rapid impressions it should give deepened expression and intensification of being.

Until 1910 the main unifying force within the Berlin Secession remained sheer self-preservation. This was a country where a Social Democrat, Südehum, had declared in the Reichstag in 1904: 'And we beg to decline a republic of art with Wilhelm II at its head.' The Secession's members included Barlach, Beckmann, Feininger, Kandinsky, Kollwitz, Munch, Nolde, Amiet, Bonnard, Denis, Matisse and Rohlfs, and its guest exhibitors included the Fauves, the Brücke, members of the Munich Neue Künstlervereinigung, and, after 1911, Braque, Dufy and Picasso.

But the young members were in a small minority, and it suited the older members that this should be so. The crisis came in 1910. The initial cause was the election of Beckmann to the committee. Then the President, Liebermann, was called upon to resign by Nolde, who was consequently expelled. And finally twenty-seven of the artists rejected for the annual exhibition in 1910 arranged their own exhibition which led, on the initiative of Pechstein, to the foundation of the Neue Sezession. Fifteen artists joined it, including all the members of the Brücke, Nolde and Rohlfs. The preface to the catalogue of the third exhibition of the Neue Sezession, held in the spring of 1911, stated its programme:

Decoration, derived from Impressionism's idea of colour: that is the programme of young artists in every country; i.e. they no longer take their rules from the object, of which it was the ambition of the Impressionists to obtain an impression with the means of pure painting, but instead they think of the wall and for the wall, and in terms of colour. . . . Areas of colour are placed side by side in such a way that the incalculable laws of balance imposed by colour quantities abrogate the rigid, scientific laws of colour qualities with a new personal freedom of movement and expansion of available space. These areas of colour do not destroy the basic lines of the objects represented, but line is once more consciously used as a factor, not to express or shape forms, but to describe forms, to characterize the expression of a feeling and to place figurative life firmly on the surface. . . . Each and every object is only the channel of a colour, a colour composition, and the work as a whole aims, not at an impression of nature, but at the expression of feelings. Science and imitation disappear once more in favour of original creation.

The fourth exhibition, which opened in November 1911, and of which Nolde was to write: 'There was no more concentrated assembly of the best works of our young art in the following twenty years', was already the last of significance. The Brücke left the Neue Sezession because the majority of the members were not sufficiently gifted to be able to carry out a visible separation of 'past and future'. The Neue Sezession collapsed as a result. Pechstein rejoined the old Secession at once, while the other members of the Brücke exhibited there again in 1913. In 1912 the remaining members of the Neue Sezession turned to Herwarth Walden, who had become the principal advocate of progressive art in Berlin.

The Secession itself split up again for the last time in 1913, when the majority of its members left to re-form as the Freie ('free') Sezession. Paul Cassirer persuaded reluctant artists into the exhibition by buying the pictures they were prepared to exhibit. This helped the very first exhibition of the Freie Sezession, in 1914, to eliminate a possible rival, Walden's Herbstsalon.

Walden had founded *Der Sturm* in March 1910, a weekly, championing the new movements in art, which was very soon selling thirty thousand copies. The first artist Walden promoted in the magazine was his collaborator, the Viennese painter-draughtsman Oskar *123* Kokoschka; then came the Brücke group. But it was not until 1912 that Walden was in a position to stage exhibitions. He opened his gallery with the first exhibition of the Blauer Reiter and Kokoschka.

Already the second, at which he showed the Futurists, was so successful that there were sometimes as many as a thousand visitors in a day. The exhibitions changed every month, and there were a hundred by 1921, all devoted to the European avant-garde, and accompanied by vehement propaganda in *Der Sturm*.

Artists were often irritated by Walden's high-powered salesmanship. Macke wrote to Marc in 1912: 'The racket he makes pushing the associations and advertising is terrible. I shall soon be sick of *Der Sturm* and the eternal manifestos.' Klee wrote in his diary in 1912:

> Once again, the very next day, there was an opportunity of watching little Herwarth Walden while the Futurists were being hung in the Galerie Thannhauser. Lives on cigarettes, gives orders and dashes about like a strategist. He is somebody; but there's something missing. He doesn't even care for the pictures in the least! He just has a good nose for sniffing something in them.

Perhaps that was the very reason why so many of Walden's enterprises were successful, the most important of them probably being the Erster Deutscher Herbstsalon in 1913. Even though Nolde and the Brücke, among the Germans, and Braque and Picasso, among the French, for example, were missing, he still managed to present a wide spectrum of the latest in European art, with Archipenko, Arp, Baumeister, Chagall, Delaunay, Ernst, Léger, Mondrian, as well as the Expressionists, Futurists and Cubists he had shown in his earlier shows.

Financially this exhibition was a disaster, so it was not possible to repeat the undertaking. Instead, Walden organized a large number of smaller touring exhibitions, of which sometimes up to twelve were on show simultaneously, not merely in Germany but in Scandinavia, London, and even Tokyo.

Walden's propaganda machine played a decisive role in establishing the success of the new art, which he called 'Expressionism'. But at the same time it was as much a hindrance as a help, gradually driving the most important of the artists he promoted away from him. Not only had Walden opposed *Aktion*, the magazine Franz Pfempfert founded in Berlin in 1910, from its very first issue, in spite, or perhaps because, of its being an organ on the side of progressive art, though more politically oriented; he was equally energetic in his antagonism towards newer publications like *Das Kunstblatt*, whose editor Paul Westheim he could not forgive for having once taken a different attitude to various artists. Walden refused to recognize the truth of the situation, which Klee explained to him in 1916:

> About *Der Sturm* as a magazine, I would say that it is quite excellent as the organ for coming things, but it no longer serves as the representative of what is new but already established. . . . And I regret that I must also protest against the title, which is now out of date. World peace exists on the cultural front; our creed seems a storm only to old gentlemen.

MAX BECKMANN

> In my opinion there are two directions in art. One, which is the more dominant at the moment, is the art of surface and stylized decoration, the other is concerned with space and depth. . . . For myself, I pursue the art of space and depth with all my soul, and try to achieve my own style in it. I want a style that, in contrast to the art of exterior decoration, will penetrate as deeply as possible into the fundamentals of nature, into the soul of things. I am fully aware that many of the feelings I experience have already existed before. But I also recognize what is new in my feelings, what I have drawn from my time and its spirit. It is not something that I want to or can define. It is in my pictures.

Thus Max Beckmann in 1914 in the journal *Kunst und Künstler*. By then thirty years old, Beckmann was already widely recognized as a painter. A monograph on him with a catalogue of his works had appeared in the previous year. He was considered the most gifted and promising representative of the kind of painting encouraged by the Berlin Secession in the spirit of Liebermann.

The argument with Marc that Beckmann had conducted in the pages of *Pan* in 1912 had contributed to his reputation. Replying to two articles by Marc, Beckmann wrote:

> I too have something to say about quality. Quality as I understand it. Appreciation, that is, for the peach-coloured sheen of skin, the glint of a nail, for what is artistically sensual, for what it is that, in the softness of flesh, in the depth and gradation of space, lies not only on the surface but also in the depth. And then above all in the attraction of the material. The gloss of oil-paint, when I think of Rembrandt, Leibl or Cézanne, or the inspired structure of the brushstroke in Hals.

Marc replied with another article, which he headed 'Anti-Beckmann':

> No, Herr Beckmann, quality is not to be found in the glint of a nail or the gloss of oilpaint. Quality is the name given to the inner greatness of

a work, the attribute that distinguishes it from the works of imitators and small minds.

It will be clear that Beckmann took no part in his generation's search for a radical renewal of form, but was concerned instead with the conscious continuation and development of the tradition in which he had grown up. He was only fifteen years old in 1899 when he entered the academy in Weimar, where he received a sound education from the painter of portraits and genre scenes Carl Frithjof Smith. He left Weimar in 1903 and went to Paris for the first time, where he spent six months and where Impressionism, especially Manet, made a decisive impact upon him. In 1904 he moved to Berlin. The first demonstration he gave the public of his great ability was the large academic composition *Young Men Beside the Sea*, which he showed in 1906 at the exhibition of the Deutscher Künstlerbund (German League of Artists) in Weimar. Not only was the picture bought by the museum in Weimar, but it won him the Villa Romana prize, which took him to Florence for six months' study. Beckmann had submitted

124 another painting to the same exhibition, *Large Deathbed Scene*, which the jury had turned down. In it Beckmann transferred directly on to the canvas a horrific vision, probably evoked in him by his mother's death. The closeness to Munch is obvious. And it was Munch who advised the young artist at the time not to continue with the conventional type of classicist figure composition, since the *Large Deathbed Scene* showed that he was capable of more important things.

It remained an isolated outburst, but it showed that Beckmann was not after all so very far removed from his contemporaries. Curt Glaser wrote in 1924: 'Beckmann is one of those artists who are compelled to communicate. He is an "Expressionist", not by virtue of his form, but by virtue of this inner compulsion.'

Beckmann adopted history painting as his means of expression. In 1906 he painted a crucifixion with the title *Drama*. The great Delacroix exhibition held in Berlin in the same year confirmed and encouraged him in his chosen course. On large canvases, which sometimes measured more than six feet by ten, he painted battle scenes, a crucifixion, the descent of the Holy Ghost, Christ bearing the Cross, or subjects like Adam and Eve, Venus and Mars, or Samson and Delilah; he experimented with the depiction of recent events, as in the *Messina Earthquake* of 1910 or the *Sinking of the Titanic* of 1912. He also painted landscapes, usually in smaller formats, and portraits. But the occasions

124 MAX BECKMANN *Large Deathbed Scene* 1906

on which he succeeded in penetrating to 'the soul of things' were rare; his formal means were not appropriate to the task. He himself must have known this, for after a very prolific year in 1913 he painted very little in 1914.

At the outbreak of war Beckmann volunteered for service in the medical corps. He was posted first of all to East Prussia, then to Flanders, where he met Heckel. In the proximity of horror and death, which he was not able to endure for more than a year, Beckmann found himself. Surface gloss ceased to interest him. He wrote to his wife in 1915: 'I hope that I shall gradually be able to get simpler, increasingly concentrated in my expression, but I shall never, I know, abandon the fullness, the roundness, the pulse of life, on the contrary, I should like to intensify it more and more – you know what I mean by intensified roundness: no arabesques, no calligraphy, but volume and plasticity.'

After a nervous breakdown in 1915 Beckmann was released from the service. He made his break with the past a complete one, not merely in his work but in his personal life as well. He left his wife and settled in Frankfurt. But it was a long time before he was able to exorcize his horror and fear in drawing and painting, to make himself *129* safe against death and danger. The *Self-portrait with a Red Scarf* of 1917 shows Beckmann as a man tormented and pursued, a figure apparently unable to stand upright, supporting himself with difficulty by leaning against the edge of the picture.

Beckmann had said of Heinrich von Kleist: 'Just think what he might have been able to achieve, if he had been tougher.' Beckmann was tougher. He resumed painting in the subject-field that had preoccupied him before the war. In 1916 he began a monumental *Resurrection*, which remained unfinished, and in 1917 he painted *125* *Christ and the Woman Taken in Adultery* and a *Deposition*. The whole of his virtuoso technique is thrown overboard in these paintings. Their construction is based on their drawing, in which Beckmann exercised himself at this period in numerous graphics, cycles and single works. The colouring is reduced to cool local colours. The whole picture plane is filled by sharp, angular forms, pressed violently against each other: the order imposed by linear or aerial perspective is missing. But Beckmann remained loyal to 'the art of space and depth'. He wrote later: 'For in the beginning was space, this mysterious, intellectually incomprehensible invention. Time is an invention of man, space is the palace of the gods.' He had already noted in 1915:

> This infinite space, whose foreground has always got to be filled with some rubbish or other, so as to disguise its dreadful depths. What would we poor human creatures do if we weren't always ready to summon up an idea – fatherland, love, art, religion – to cover over just a little bit of the dark black hole. This sense of being abandoned endlessly in eternity. This loneliness.

To solve the problem that space represented to him, Beckmann turned to medieval precedents, whose *horror vacui* he shared. It is relevant that

164

125 MAX BECKMANN *Deposition* 1917

the work that made the strongest impression on him in Paris in 1903 was not by one of his contemporaries at all, but the *Pietà* of the Master of Avignon.

'If one can look at all of this – the whole business of the war, or even the whole of life as just one scene in the drama of eternity, a lot of things become easier to endure.' One such scene is the horrifying nightmare of torture and murder, to which he gave the title of *The*

126 *Night* (1918–19). It was a subject he had tackled before in an etching of 1914. Fear, torment, loneliness are also the dominant traits of the
127 rare landscapes of the years following the war, like the *Synagogue* of 1919.

  The world appears as a grotesque, joyless harlequinade beneath too bright a spotlight in Beckmann's pictures of the years up to 1923, such
130, 128 as *Carnival* of 1920 or *Before the Masked Ball* of 1922. The figures seem to lack a relationship; they seem not to know what to do with the countless props. The stern, static arrangement of pictures like these, the cool style of representation, the way detail is used to clarify the object, illustrate Beckmann's overriding desire to contain his urgent feelings within himself, to control the expressive forces.

  There is nothing I hate so much as sentimentality. The stronger and more intense my wish to record the inexpressible things of life becomes, and

126 MAX BECKMANN *The Night* 1918

127 MAX BECKMANN *The Synagogue* 1919

the more heavily and deeply distress over our existence burns in me, the more tightly I close my mouth, the cooler my desire becomes to seize this frightful twitching monster of vitality and to cage it in glass-clear sharp lines and surfaces, to suppress it, to throttle it. I do not weep, I hate tears as a sign of slavery. I always concentrate on the essential thing.

On a leg, an arm, on the marvellous sense of foreshortening breaking through the surface, on the division of the space, on the combination of the straight lines in relation to the crooked ones. . . . Roundness in a surface, depth in the feeling of a surface, the architecture of a picture.

Piety! God? O beautiful word, so much misused. I am both, if I shall so have done my work that I can at last die. A painted or a drawn hand, a grinning or weeping face, that is my credo; if I have felt something of life, it is in that. . . .

LYONEL FEININGER

In 1917 Herwarth Walden put on the first collective exhibition of Lyonel Feininger's work in the Sturm gallery, showing a total of 111 paintings. The exhibition was the turning-point of the forty-six-year-old artist's life, as he said himself. He received overnight recognition as a painter. Less than two years later, in 1919, he was the first person appointed to the staff of the Bauhaus in Weimar.

Feininger was previously well known as one of the most famous political cartoonists in Berlin. Since 1894, after leaving art school in Berlin, he had been contributing to the satirical weeklies *Lustige Blätter* and *Ulk*, to the supplement to the daily *Berliner Tageblatt*, and later to *Das Narrenschiff* and *Sporthumor* as well. He was so extraordinarily successful that as early as 1901 Georg Herrmann wrote in his *Die deutsche Karikatur im 19. Jahrhundert*: 'Lyonel Feininger is the first among the Berlin graphic artists.'

The need to get away from drawing cartoons began to weigh on Feininger from 1905 onwards. 'I'm barely an artist,' he wrote; 'at any rate, not in the tomfool jokes that I'm known for.' It was at that period that he discovered the scenery of Weimar and Thuringia, which was to be a source of material to him for decades. He described the fascination that he wanted to depict in a letter to his wife in 1905.

The picture before my eyes every morning . . . the houses in front of me, and to right and left, as far as my field of vision reaches, still cool in the shadows low down, already getting warmer higher up. Windows reflect, yawning and dark low down, silver above; and at the very top, in the roofs, where they reflect the blue sky, they are deep blue. And the top story of this long cliff of façades is lit with so deep a golden glow, by the sun, which is then reflected back on to my table, on to this sheet of paper, which shimmers like an opal in shades of gold and purple – and above the strip of gold on the upper floor of the houses, a turquoise-blue sky, so beautiful as to bring tears to your eyes. Every day, every day now. . . . Reflecting windows – no one has ever suggested this to me, this is all mine, and I give it to you . . . reflecting windows. Even when I was a little boy, in the country, how much I loved them. There will be a whole cycle of works in it! Sunset, everything in gold and purple half-tones, and in one spot, right in the very far distance, half hidden by trees, two or three rows of windows facing west, throwing back the gold of the sky like spears, transforming the whole picture in an indescribably beautiful tone. In the already dying eastern sky, the goodnight sky, there are suddenly pieces like jewels from the sun-irradiated western sky, just put there quite frankly and impudently – I have always found this violent confrontation of two different skies quite uncannily beautiful . . . love for everything, for everything . . . at times like this I know that I am not just one of the crowd.

Feininger went to Paris in 1906, to learn the techniques he would need. He studied, as he had done before in the winter of 1892–93, in the *atelier* of the Italian sculptor Colarossi. He made friends with German artists in Matisse's circle, like Purrmann, Moll and Levi, and frequented the Café du Dôme. His stay in Paris lasted until 1908, interrupted by visits to Normandy, the Black Forest and the Baltic. Feininger experimented with constructing his pictures from the silhouettes of objects, without any kind of three-dimensional modelling, and in doing so discovered for himself the unity of object and space. It was hard for him to withdraw from 'accustomed reality', but he knew that 'what is seen must be inwardly re-formed and crystallized'.

After his return to Berlin, his experience as a cartoonist continued to affect his work markedly for several years, up to 1911. Most of Feininger's paintings at this period were of figures, transported to a world of fantasy, 'mummery pictures' as he called them himself. His use of colour clearly reveals a familiarity with the Fauves. He also sketched landscapes in homage to Van Gogh.

In 1911 he went to Paris again, for a mere two weeks, and there discovered in Cubism something of what he had intuitively been seeking for years. The crystalline or prismatic construction of his paintings of 1912, such as *Cycle Race*, serves an absolute synthesis of   132
rhythm, form, perspective and colour. Feininger wrote in 1912: 'I am trying to formulate a perspective of objects which is completely new, completely my own. I would like to put myself into the picture and look at the landscape and the objects painted from that position.' His premiss here does have a similarity to Cubism, but his goal was something quite different. His aim was not dissection but concentration.

In 1912 Feininger met the members of the Brücke, and became friendly with Schmidt-Rottluff and Heckel. He also got to know Kubin at the same time; and it was through the latter that he was invited to take part in Walden's Herbstsalon in 1913. Feininger was greatly encouraged by this exhibition. 'But the consciousness of working with others, each of whom in his own way is trying to penetrate to the most inward form of expression, is an invigorating sensation', he wrote to Kubin.

In the summer of 1913 Feininger went to Thuringia to paint; and at Gelmeroda, where he had spent time sketching in 1906, he started to work on what was really the primary theme of his whole *œuvre*.   131
'I don't suppose that I shall ever represent human subjects in the normal

128 MAX BECKMANN
Before the Masked Ball 1922

129 MAX BECKMANN
Self-portrait with a Red Scarf
1917

130 MAX BECKMANN
Carnival
1920

sense in my pictures: but on the other hand humanity is the only thing that moves me in everything. Without warm human feelings I can't do anything.' Buildings – a church, a mill, a bridge, a house – were for him images of a law, of a valid spiritual force. And if disquiet and motion were used as expressive means in these years, his search for *133* monumentality soon led to complete peace, as in the picture *Zirchow V* of 1916. 'In time,' he wrote in 1917, 'I shall probably succeed in withdrawing myself further and further from torment and fragmentation. Ultimate form can only be achieved by complete peace in a picture.' This peace is affected by a certain oppressiveness when, as in *134* *Bathers II* of 1917, Feininger depicts ships and people totally without movement, reflecting the dark shadows that the war cast on his spirit.

Notwithstanding his rejection of every kind of manifesto and grouping, Feininger was one of the few Expressionist artists who explicitly acknowledged themselves to be Expressionists. He wrote to Paul Westheim in 1917:

> Each individual work serves as an expression of our most personal state of mind at that particular moment and of the inescapable, imperative need for release by means of an appropriate act of creation: in the rhythm, form, colour and mood of a picture.

131 LYONEL
FEININGER
Gelmeroda I 1913

132 LYONEL FEININGER *Cycle Race* 1912

ERNST BARLACH

When Ernst Barlach settled in Berlin in 1905, years of restless move-ment lay behind him. He had studied in Hamburg and Dresden, spent two long periods in Paris, returned to his birthplace in Holstein, lived in Thuringia, and taught at a school of ceramics in the Wester-wald. No particular purpose or plan lay behind this peregrination, and Barlach's artistic activity was equally aimless, though he was already exercising his talents as sculptor, graphic artist and writer simul-taneously. He wrote in his diary in 1906: 'Mythic observation is to me the foundation of all art . . . creating in visions is divine art, art in a higher, and therefore better sense than the art of reality, which comes from simple technical ability. Having visions is the capacity for sensual sight.'

Barlach made his discovery of nature, which was to be the liberating experience for him, at the age of thirty-six, on a visit to Russia, which took him via Warsaw and Kiev to Kharkov and the Donets Basin in 1906. What he discovered was more than just indications of how to develop form in the direction of integrated mass. 'No, the astounding

133 LYONEL FEININGER *Zirchow V* 1916

revelation impressed itself upon me, in the words: You may freely dare everything that is yours, the utmost, the inmost, gestures of piety and gesticulations of anger, without any hesitation, for there is a means of expression for everything, whether hellish paradise or paradisal hell, one or both of which is realized in Russia.'

Russian peasants and beggars, 'whom I felt to be symbols of the human situation in its nakedness between heaven and earth', formed his thematic inspiration after his return to Berlin. Very often the motifs of his sculptures and his drawings are almost identical; for instance, the sculpture *Careworn Woman* of 1910 is very close to the woman in the lithograph *Couple in Conversation* of 1912, from the sequence *The Dead Day*.

135

174

134 LYONEL FEININGER *Bathers II* 1917

Barlach became a member of the Berlin Secession in 1906 and regularly exhibited there from 1907. Paul Cassirer made a contract with him, which relieved him of material anxieties, and in 1909 he was awarded a bursary at the Villa Romana in Florence. In 1912 Barlach's first play, *Der tote Tag* ('The Dead Day') was published by Bruno Cassirer, with its accompanying sequence of lithographs. Barlach left Berlin in 1910 and settled in Güstrow in Mecklenburg, where he lived until his death in 1938. Although in his spiritual and intellectual premisses Barlach shared so much common ground with the progressives among his contemporaries, so that he, too, could voice the demand: 'We must get away from the attitudes of the bourgeoisie! We must gain the courage to feel at home in the realm of the spirit!', yet there was also much that he instinctively rejected. Kandinsky's *Über das Geistige in der Kunst* provoked a categorical rejection from him in 1911. He was unable to allow that 'profound spiritual disturbance' could be caused by 'spots, splashes, lines and dots'. He felt that Picasso was something of a confidence trickster. He constantly reiterated his own position in this respect: 'For me the organic in nature is the expression of its inner being, the human figure is the expression of God, in so far as he broods, haunts and burrows in and behind man.' Barlach himself closed the circle when, in the last years of his life, he began to copy from works originally composed between 1908 and 1912.

LUDWIG MEIDNER

Everything he does is expression, eruption, explosion. This is the hottest crater of a volcanic epoch, spewing out the lava of its visions in un-predictable bursts and with irresistible power, in the relentless swell of the

135 ERNST BARLACH *Couple in Conversation* 1912

136 ERNST BARLACH *The Cathedrals* 1922

inner fire. There is probably no other artist whose hand is directed as absolutely as Meidner's by the will to give tongue to his latent explosiveness, the vaulting of his spiritual urgings, his furious energies, to force, to hurl out his inmost being on canvas and paper. A violent passion to disclose himself, a wildness in comprehension that is like a sudden attack, an exultant dissipation of convulsive strength, a heart well acquainted with ecstasy and relentless driving needs: and all this, aflame, casts its glow into the face of the onlooker with uncanny force, and again and again the intact rocklike genius of his awkward, angular personality, unconsumed by the flame, bursts open and is revealed to the fascinated gaze.

When Willi Wolfradt wrote that about Ludwig Meidner in 1920, he was, without knowing it, writing Meidner's epitaph as an Expressionist. The volcanic, ecstatic painter and writer fell silent almost as suddenly as he had appeared on the scene in 1912, although he did not give up painting and writing.

137

137 LUDWIG MEIDNER
Self-portrait 1915

138 LUDWIG MEIDNER
Apocalyptic Landscape c. 1913

The eighth exhibition Herwarth Walden put on in the Sturm gallery, in November 1912, was called 'Die Pathetiker' ('The Passionate'), a group which Ludwig Meidner, Jakob Steinhardt and Richard Janthur had formed in the spring. For Meidner, as for others, the exhibition of his works by the Sturm was a turning-point. He had attended the academy at Breslau from 1903 to 1905 and had then gone to Berlin, where he scraped a living as a fashion artist. In 1906 a private bursary enabled him to go to Paris, to study at the Académie Julian. He remained unaffected by artistic controversies. The only person with whom he cultivated a close relationship was Modigliani, who painted several portraits of him, one of which he showed at the Salon d'Automne in 1907. Meidner returned to Berlin in 1907, where he eked out a penurious existence until 1911. Then he gained some relief from a small award, made on the recommendation of Max Beckmann. The Sturm's exhibitions of Futurists, Cubists and, above all, of Delaunay encouraged Meidner to give free rein to his passionate nature. In 1912 the twenty-eight-year-old artist began suddenly to express himself in visions and ecstasies, unrestrained by any formal considerations. Characteristically, Meidner's prolific literary output contains no mention of artistic problems; it is all concerned with his 'inner condition'. It was probably for that reason that he was very soon more at home among writers and poets than with painters.

Meidner was able to maintain his pace for a bare ten years. Like so many of his writer friends, he could not develop his form any further, in spite of an apparent success in the years immediately following the war. Finally, in 1923, he recanted:

> The spleen, the excess and the shamelessness which used to flourish in my earlier prose-writings, I have now left far, far behind me, and my faith in God has so much purified and sobered me that today it is only with the deepest blushes that I can read my youthful works.

OSKAR KOKOSCHKA

Kokoschka describes his life in Berlin in a later article, 'Aus meinem dreissigjährigen Emigrantenleben als deutscher Künstler' ('My Thirty Years of Exile as a German Artist'):

> It was at that time [1910] that I emigrated to the Hohenzollerns' Berlin, where the Siegesallee had just been finished, and with Herwarth Walden I founded the first German magazine for contemporary art. I was its graphic artist, poet, theatre critic, advertising manager and distributor

all rolled into one. Man does not live by bread alone. But no one can fill his stomach by the word alone, even in the German empire. I had plenty of opportunity to learn that, in my *Sturm und Drang* period, when I was painting that whole series of pictures that art lovers later gave to museums. On several occasions I didn't even get to sign my pictures, and abandoned picture and paint-box, because at the last minute I always had inhibitions about selling my work. Finding a new paint-box, in particular, was always a problem. I would damned well have liked to learn the secret of how to remain a free artist without starving; there were so many winter days when I pressed my nose to the frozen window panes of the Romanisches Café, where the academicians were holding debates about art. I knew more about painting than they did, but I never had any money.

Kokoschka's introduction to Herwarth Walden in 1910 was due to the Viennese architect Adolf Loos, to whose encouragement he owed much. At the age of nineteen, in 1905, Kokoschka had won a bursary enabling him to study at the Kunstgewerbeschule in Vienna, with the intention of becoming a teacher. This choice of profession was determined not so much by a long-standing wish – at that time Kokoschka would have much preferred to become a research chemist – as by the opportunity of taking the bursary.

The Kunstgewerbeschule was oriented solely towards ornamental and decorative art. 'Nothing but leaves and flowers and stems, twisting about like dragons. Drawing the human figure was taboo.' Kokoschka learned drawing, lithography, calligraphy, bookbinding and other crafts, but not painting. In that, he had to find his own way, self-taught. A Van Gogh exhibition in 1906 made a deep impression on him, as his earliest surviving work, *Still-life with Pineapple* of 1907, shows. But the art of the Far East interested him more, and of course he had to come to terms with Gustav Klimt, the dominant figure in Viennese painting. Kokoschka admired Klimt greatly, and in drawing adopted his strictly linear style, without shading, but aimed at the stronger sense of movement that he saw in Japanese woodcuts.

139

> What I learned from them is precise, fast observation of movement – the Japanese have got the fastest eyes in the whole history of painting, every horse in their pictures jumps correctly, every butterfly settles correctly on its petal, every woodcutter swings his axe correctly, absolutely every movement of men and beasts is reproduced exactly as it should be. Movement! But movement exists only in space, in three-dimensional space.

139 OSKAR KOKOSCHKA
Still-life with Pineapple
c. 1907

140 OSKAR KOKOSCHKA Drawing
for *Mörder Hoffnung der Frauen*
c. 1908

Kokoschka preferred to work with the thinnest possible models, skinny circus children, 'because you can see their joints, sinews and muscles so clearly, and because the effect of each movement is modelled more emphatically with them'.

In 1907 Kokoschka joined the Wiener Werkstätte (Vienna Workshops), founded by Josef Hoffmann in 1903, where he spent time painting fans, bookbinding and similar activities. One advantage that came of being a member of the Wiener Werkstätte was the opportunity to take part in the Kunstschau of 1908, the most important exhibition held in Vienna before the First World War. He exhibited large tapestry designs as well as a picture book, *Die träumenden Knaben* ('The Dreaming Youths'), published by the Wiener Werkstätte and dedicated to Klimt; this still owed a great deal to Jugendstil influence.

141 OSKAR
KOKOSCHKA
Auguste Forel
c. 1909

142 OSKAR
KOKOSCHKA
Herwarth Walden
1910

140   Kokoschka also designed a memorable poster for his own play *Mörder Hoffnung der Frauen* ('Murderer, the Women's Hope'), which received its first performance, at the open-air theatre adjoining the Kunstschau, in 1909, and caused a great furore.

    It was the Kunstschau that first called Kokoschka to the attention of Adolf Loos, who promised to solicit commissions for him and guaranteed to maintain his income at its current level if he would leave the Wiener Werkstätte. Loos also introduced him to the literary circle which centred on the poets Karl Kraus (editor of the magazine *Die Fackel*) and Peter Altenberg, both of whom he painted. In 1909 he left both the Kunstgewerbeschule and the Wiener Werkstätte; but in spite of all his friends' efforts to find him work, he found it impossible to make a living. He went to Switzerland to paint the portraits of 141   Frau Loos and of the biologist Professor Forel, but nobody would have the pictures. The Forel family refused to buy the professor's portrait on the grounds that it did not look like their father. Two years later, however, after a stroke, Forel gradually began to look more like the portrait. In portraits like these Kokoschka laid the soul

182

bare, and what was revealed was not beautiful. In the drawings illustrating *Mörder Hoffnung der Frauen* he made the nerves of his characters visible as if they lay on the surface of the skin, because he was himself always in pain from neuralgia; in the same way, in his portraits, he projected his own anguish, his own torment on to his sitters, which gave his conception of them a positively hallucinatory quality. Kokoschka called this projection of himself the fourth dimension, based on the creative nature of seeing, while the other three dimensions derived from mere eyesight. Karl Kraus acknowledged this when he wrote in *Die Fackel*:

> My vanity, which does not concern itself with my body, would be glad to recognize itself in a monster, if it recognized the spirit of the artist in it, and I am proud of a Kokoschka's testimony, because the truth of the genius that distorts is higher than the truth of anatomy, and because in the presence of art reality is only an optical illusion.

After his move to Berlin in 1910, Kokoschka continued to paint more portraits than anything else; some of them, as well as the drawings for *Mörder Hoffnung der Frauen*, were reproduced in *Der Sturm*. Even though his period in Berlin did nothing to alleviate his financial straits, Kokoschka's name became widely known through *Der Sturm*. Paul Cassirer showed the first collective exhibition of his work, which later

142

143 OSKAR KOKOSCHKA *The Temptation of Christ* 1911–12

144 OSKAR KOKOSCHKA *Landscape in the Dolomites: Tre Croci* 1913

moved to the Folkwang-Museum in Hagen, and in 1910 gave him his first contract, guaranteeing to buy one picture a year.

Although Kokoschka returned to Vienna in the spring of 1911, he remained better known in Germany, where he contributed to every exhibition of importance: those of the Sturm gallery and the Secession in Berlin, the Sonderbund in Cologne and the Neue Sezession in Munich. He contributed to the Blauer Reiter almanac, and a volume of his plays and pictures was published for the first time in Leipzig in 1913. In Vienna, on the other hand, he was received with nothing but malice and rejection when he showed twenty-five pictures at the Hagenbund exhibition in 1911. It was many years before his work was shown again in Vienna.

For a time Kokoschka's interest shifted from portraiture to figure composition, especially in religious subjects, to which he added landscape backgrounds. In order to take a firm grasp of the spatial dimensions, he painted a prismatic network of coloured lines and planes over the surface of his pictures. In this, he was experiencing colour not

185

145 OSKAR KOKOSCHKA *The Bride of the Wind (The Tempest)* 1914

merely as the means of giving shape to space, not merely as an expressive medium, but as a sensual element. When he went to Italy with his mistress Alma Mahler in 1913, the Venetian masters, Veronese, Titian and Tintoretto, confirmed the validity of the experience. The first work showing the effect of this is the landscape *Tre Croci*, which displays the density of colour and unity of space that remained fundamental characteristics of his work.

144

The most important picture of this period is *The Bride of the Wind* (*The Tempest*) of 1914, a work which achieves a monumental force of expression solely by means of colour.

145

Kokoschka volunteered for military service at the outbreak of war and was seriously wounded in 1915. From 1917 onwards he lived in Dresden, at first still as a convalescent. The pictures which he painted at this period are all characterized by a nervy, rather fidgety handling,

186

which demonstrates the severe struggle he had with the physical and psychological effects of his injuries. He projected his own inner conflicts in group portraits of his friends, such as *The Emigrés* of 1916–17. To the Viennese art historian Hans Tietze he wrote:

> There was a time when I knew how to evoke the essence of a person, let's say his 'daemon', with such elemental simplicity, that the one principal line made one forget the chance elements that were omitted. . . . I brought it off on some occasions, and the result was 'a person', in the way that the picture one forms of one's friends in one's memory is more vivid in its effect than the actual sight of them is, because it's concentrated, as if by a lens, and therefore is capable of radiating. . . . What I'm doing now is to construct compositions from human faces (models like the people who happen to have been sticking it out with me here for a long time now, people who know me, and whom I know inside and out, with the result that they virtually haunt me, like nightmares), and in these compositions entities conflict, oppose each other rigidly, like hate and love, and in each picture I'm looking for the dramatic 'accident' which will weld the individual spirits into a higher order. The picture I painted last year that you liked, *The Emigrés*, was one such, and at the moment there

146

146 OSKAR KOKOSCHKA *The Emigrés* 1916–17

is one called *The Gamblers* which I started five months ago and am at last near to finishing. The figures in it are my friends playing cards. Each of them indulging his passion, horrifyingly naked, and all plunged in a colouring of a higher order, which binds them together in the way light raises an object and its mirror-image into a category which has something of the reality and something of the reflection and therefore more of both.

Kokoschka was appointed professor at the Akademie der Bildenden Künste (Academy of Fine Arts) in Dresden in 1919, but while his external situation became more stable he still did not succeed in escaping from human isolation. To alleviate his despair he had a life-size doll made, to serve as companion and model. He painted it over 147 and over again, as in *Woman in Blue* of 1919. The paint is applied without thinning, with a thick brush and palette knife. With concentration Kokoschka managed to subdue the graphic element and to return to construction by means of colour.

He remained in Dresden until 1924. Then he suddenly left the academy and the city without taking any formal leave. Paris became his base in the ensuing years, and he travelled extensively.

147 OSKAR KOKOSCHKA *Woman in Blue c.* 1919

148 OSKAR KOKOSCHKA *Neustadt, Dresden c.* 1922

EGON SCHIELE

The year was 1913. It's important to know what Berlin signified to us in Vienna at that time, everything, really. Berlin was for us infamous, corrupt, metropolitan, anonymous, gigantic, pregnant with the future, literary, political, artistic (as the city for artists): in short, hell-hole and paradise in one. I went for a walk with one of my friends on the Gloriette hill behind Vienna. It was night. There was a glow in the sky to the north. 'Berlin's over there', I said. 'We must go to Berlin', I said.

The words are those of the writer Hans Flesch von Brunningen, who, like Schiele, contributed to the Berlin weekly *Die Aktion*, which published a drawing of him by Schiele. Schiele himself wrote in 1914: 'We must never wish to have the past back again, that would be retreat. Therefore I don't want to stay here with you – but to go to Berlin after the war and find the courage to start to live again.' He was sure that he would be able to make the move by autumn 1915 at the latest, but was prevented from doing so by conscription.

Schiele had been quick to gain recognition in Germany. He had joined the Munich group Sema, to which Klee and Kubin also belonged, in 1911. In 1912, when he was still only twenty-two, Hans

149 EGON SCHIELE *Embrace* 1917

Goltz's Galerie Neue Kunst in Munich, where the second Blauer Reiter exhibition was held, gave him a contract. Schiele was represented in the Sonderbund exhibition in Cologne, regularly participated in the Munich Secession, and had collective exhibitions in Munich, Dresden, Stuttgart, Berlin, Breslau, Hamburg and Hagen (at the Folkwang-Museum), before he got the opportunity for one in Vienna. In 1916 *Die Aktion* in Berlin published a supplement on him.

But although Schiele complained in 1910, 'I wish I could leave Vienna, very soon. How vile it is – everyone envies me and wants to do me down', he was not totally unappreciated there. He had had opportunities of exhibiting since 1909, when he was still a student, and could rely on a loyal circle of friends and buyers. He took part in official Austrian exhibitions in Amsterdam, Copenhagen and Stockholm, and in 1917, together with Gustav Klimt, became one of the founders of the Kunsthalle ('Hall of art'), the aim of which was 'that the flight of talent abroad should cease, and that all those whom Austria has produced should be able to work to Austria's honour'. Schiele's relationship with Klimt was very important to him, progressing from the dependence of a pupil to an admiring friendship, which

150 CHRISTIAN ROHLFS *Return of the Prodigal Son* 1914–15

151 EGON SCHIELE
Self-portrait 1910

152 EGON SCHIELE
Death Agony 1912

he commemorated in the painting *The Hermits* of 1912. Schiele, who attended the Vienna art academy from 1906 to 1909, came very much under Klimt's influence in 1908–09. But he was soon able to bring a more ascetic attitude of his own to bear in his portraits, as a counterpoise to the elegance of Klimt's figures and the harmonious, decorative way they are blended into the picture plane. Schiele sets his figures against a bare background, without associations, and his handling is more temperate and austere; it seems more closely related to Kokoschka's illustrations for *Die träumenden Knaben* of 1908.

After leaving art school, Schiele founded the Neukunstgruppe (New Art Group) with Gütersloh, Peschka and Faistauer. On the occasion of an exhibition by the group in Vienna in 1910, he noted:

Art is always the same thing: art. Therefore there is no 'new art'. But, there are new artists. Even a study by a new artist is always a work of

art; it is a piece of himself that is alive. . . . The new artist must be un-conditionally himself; he must be a creator; without needing all the relics of tradition and the past, he must have in himself, immediate and entire, the foundation on which he builds.

The immediacy of which Schiele wrote, and his own sense of menace, fear and pain, are visible in tense, tormented figures like the *Self-*   *151* *portrait* of 1910. Their bodies are out of joint and doubled-up, limbs painfully twisted, fingers compulsively outstretched, like some of the trees in his lonely landscapes.

Schiele was very conscious of the threatened condition of existence. 'I am a human being, I love death and I love life.' Growth and decay, life and death preoccupied him in numerous pictures in the years that followed, like *Death Agony* of 1912, and prompted him to paint a   *152* series of religious subjects.

Human figures and portraits are the principal themes of Schiele's drawings, while landscapes occupy a large part of his output on canvas. There are no animals or human beings in these landscapes; the trees are usually bare, apparently dead or dying. There are silent, deserted towns and villages, seen from above at a precipitate angle. These paintings rarely depict actual places; most of them come into the category of 'visions of landscape', based on any number of different sketches.

153

The eroticism that is so prominent a theme of Schiele's watercolours and drawings is rarely found in the paintings. A picture like *The Embrace* of 1917 shows none of the direct and conscious pungency in drawing which was responsible, in 1912, for Schiele's arrest on a charge of producing pornographic pictures. The physical proportions are closer to nature than in the earlier works, the outline traced more softly, in contrast to the way the sheet is made up of numerous small sections. It is clear that the artist's excitement and nervous tension is dying away, and this is also demonstrated by the change in the relationship of man to the world about him. The landscapes are

149

153 EGON SCHIELE *Landscape, Krumau* 1916

154 EGON SCHIELE *The Family* 1917

peopled now, and the setting, the room, comes to play a part in the
characterization of the subject in the portraits.

The progress Schiele had made in a few short years is clearly revealed
in his last painting, *The Family*, begun in 1917 and unfinished.   *154*
Schiele's friend Faistauer wrote in 1923:

> Here for the first time a human face looks out from one of Schiele's
> paintings. The woman's look is profoundly arresting. Her body is strongly
> built, the human organism is at work in her, her breast arches over a
> heart that beats. Which of his earlier pictures would ever have made one
> think of lungs and hearts? Here life has suddenly acquired force and built
> a body round itself which is capable of supporting a life, a body swelling
> with life, and organs from which the soul looks out mysteriously.

This picture was included in the collective exhibition at the Vienna
Secession in 1918, which was so successful that for the first time
Schiele's future seemed financially secure. He died on 31 October 1918.

If the role played by Dresden, Munich and Berlin was of vital importance to the development of progressive art in Germany after 1905, the Rhineland had an equally decisive effect on its recognition and acceptance. Hagen in Westphalia was the home of Karl Ernst Osthaus, who inherited a large fortune and at the age of twenty-four began to build the museum which was opened in 1902 as the Folkwang (Folk Hall). It included a gallery of modern art, an arts and crafts collection, and a scientific collection. When Osthaus enlisted the aid of Henry van de Velde in finishing the construction of the museum, in 1900, he wrote: 'I am busy founding a museum which is intended to win this artforsaken industrial region on the Ruhr for modern art.' At a conference organized by the Centralstelle für Arbeiter-Wohlfahrtseinrichtungen (Worker Welfare Centre) in 1903, he declared:

> But culture is not a class question today, it is a question that concerns the nation as a whole, it is the great question of our age. . . . It would certainly be a resounding success if ten thousand workers could be brought to study and appreciate the artistic treasures piled up in a museum. But what is the use of being aroused to awareness of the misery of one's daily environment, if one is not in a position to change it? . . . The question of whether we will have a culture does not depend on a majority but on those who set the standards; and in the institution I have set up, since resources are not enough to make an impression on everyone, I have decided to try to make an impression on those who have the most influence on people and events.

In 1903 Osthaus already owned three Gauguins; by 1904 he had seven. In 1905 he added six Van Goghs; in 1906 he bought Cézannes, in 1907 Matisses and Munchs. By 1912 he could observe with pride that these pictures had made a decisive contribution to the arousal of interest and understanding of the leaders of modern art in Germany.

Osthaus's efforts were seconded in Düsseldorf, where some young artists, under the inspiration of Impressionism, founded the Sonderbund Westdeutscher Kunstfreunde und Künstler (Special League of Art-lovers and Artists in Western Germany). The Sonderbund's first exhibition was held in Düsseldorf in 1909. In order to make the intention quite plain, pictures by German and French artists were hung alternately. As the Sonderbund's full name shows, the artists among its members were outnumbered by the 'art-lovers', that is, museum officials, writers, dealers and collectors. It was this combination that made the Sonderbund so effective. Osthaus was its first president.

The second Sonderbund exhibition, in 1910, again held in Düsseldorf, showed the work of the young generation of artists in Germany and France. Besides Rhineland artists, the Brücke, Kandinsky and Jawlensky were shown, while France was represented by, among others, Signac, Vuillard, Bonnard, the Fauves and Picasso. A similar exhibition was again mounted in 1911. The controversy and lack of comprehension, which were as much in evidence in Düsseldorf as they were in Berlin, Dresden or Munich, were expressed most violently in 1911 in the *Protest deutscher Künstler* ('German Artists' Protest'), published by Karl Vinnen with the backing of numerous German academics. They criticized, most strongly, the allegedly excessive value put on French art by German museum directors and collectors and a polemic against the Sonderbund exhibition of 1910 was not the least important part of the text.

The *Protest* was followed in turn by an answer, with contributions from gallery directors, artists, writers, dealers and collectors. This was found so helpful in clarifying the situation in art around 1910, that by 1913 it had gone into its third edition.

The *Protest deutscher Künstler* did, however, bring about a clearer recognition of the need for exhibitions to give not only a cross-section of current activity in art but also a survey of developments since Van Gogh, Cézanne and Gauguin. This recognition resulted in the Sonderbund's international exhibition in Cologne in 1912. With this exhibition the Sonderbund had fulfilled its purpose, and it was dissolved in 1913. Some of the founder members of the Sonderbund regrouped as Die Friedfertigen ('The Peacelovers'), while the Blauer Reiter sought a new platform in Berlin, with the aid of Herwarth Walden. Only the Brücke tried to keep the Sonderbund alive, and refused to take part in Walden's 1913 Herbstsalon in Berlin. The extent of the influence of the Sonderbund's 1912 exhibition can be seen in the fact that the Armory Show in New York in 1913, originally conceived as an exhibition of American art, was reorganized after the model of the Cologne exhibition, and became equally celebrated as a result.

The greater degree of interest in progressive art, which the Sonderbund exhibition brought about, was sustained by the efforts of the artists themselves, some of whom exhibited in Bonn in 1913 under

155 HEINRICH NAUEN *In the Garden* 1913

the title 'Rheinische Expressionisten'. Macke and Campendonk kept
the Blauer Reiter's Rhineland connections alive, while Heinrich
155, 156 Nauen, who was born in 1880 and lived in Dilborn on the lower
Rhine, and who had worked in Berlin from 1906 to 1911, retained his
connections with the Brücke and the Neue Sezession. Nauen was
much influenced by Matisse, and tried to organize his large pictures,
which involved large numbers of figures, in a calm, harmonious
rhythm. He is typical of those Rhineland artists in whose work the
combination of French and German influences is especially clear.

Another who exhibited with the Sonderbund in 1909 and 1910 was
150, 157 Christian Rohlfs, who was at the same time a member of the Neue

198

156 HEINRICH NAUEN *The Good Samaritan* 1914

157 CHRISTIAN ROHLFS *Red Roofs Beneath Trees* 1913

Sezession in Berlin. In 1901, at the age of fifty-two, Rohlfs had gone to Hagen at Osthaus's invitation. He had lived in Weimar for thirty years, painting intimate, realistic landscapes. In the stimulating atmosphere of the Folkwang-Museum he made a rapid progress through Post-Impressionism, Van Gogh and Monet. In 1906 he went to Soest in Westphalia to paint, at the same time that Nolde was there; Soest was to inspire some of the most beautiful of Rohlfs's landscapes in the following decades. He was over sixty when he discovered the style that suited him, a matter of spreading pure colours thinly and insubstantially over his surface and giving them movement by an apparently coarse, discontinuous brushwork.

Besides the ageing Rohlfs, Soest also attracted one of the greatest talents among the younger artists, Wilhelm Morgner, born in 1891, who was killed in Flanders in 1917. He was a pupil of Georg Tappert,

158

158 WILHELM MORGNER *Astral Composition XIV* 1912

who was a member of the Neue Sezession, and it was thanks to
Tappert that he exhibited at the Neue Sezession himself in 1911. He
later took part in the second Blauer Reiter exhibition and the 1912
exhibition of the Sonderbund. His woodcuts were reproduced in
Der Sturm. Under the influence of Jawlensky and Kandinsky, Morgner
felt his way towards abstraction as a means of expressing his passionate
feelings about his relationship to the world. He wrote in 1912:

> My medium of expression is colour. By means of correct composition in
> colour, I want to communicate the living god in me, directly. Not by
> shading and modifying colours, however, but by purposeful juxtaposi-
> tion of masculine and feminine colours. Light does not exist for me
> any more.

Morgner was conscripted in 1913, and never had the opportunity to
fulfil his ideas.

159 LOVIS CORINTH *The Red Christ* 1922

CHAPTER FIVE

After the War

'Victorious Expressionism', as Walden and Kandinsky called it, did not merely seize hold of the rising generation but had an equally strong effect on some older artists. One of these was Lovis Corinth, *162* born in 1858. He worked with incredible energy and vitality – his aim was once declared to be 'Leibl, painted with Teutonic fury' – until a stroke nearly killed him in 1911. The consequences of this illness acted on him as a constant *memento mori*, finally leading him to the avowal that 'true art is the exercise of unreality'. Optical impressions continued to be the prime inspiration of his work, but his forms took on an increasingly intensified expressiveness, reaching its climax in *The Red* *159* *Christ* of 1922, in which Nolde's religious visions find a common ground with Corinth's own expression of the experience of suffering. Corinth, who had taught the younger generation – August Macke was one of his pupils – was in turn inspired by that generation, probably by Kokoschka and Beckmann above all, to abandon Impressionism.

For younger artists like Otto Dix, Expressionism was the prelude *160, 161* to other things. Dix had entered the Kunstgewerbeschule in Dresden in 1909, and in the years leading up to the outbreak of war he absorbed the influences of the Brücke, the Blauer Reiter, Cubism and Futurism. He was deeply impressed by a Van Gogh exhibition held in Dresden in 1913. When war was declared he volunteered for active service, in the belief that it was an experience he needed to undergo. He portrayed the war as he saw it in hundreds of works, mostly drawings, which had the character of ecstatic visions where Dix himself appeared as Mars. The forms break up naturally into Cubist elements, the aggressiveness praised by the Futurists emerges without apparent effort. It has been said rightly that Dix's war pictures gave Futurism its true theme, beside which the Italians' subject-matter appears inadequate and forced. His war experiences continued to be the most important subject for Dix in the following decades. But after the Armistice passion had to yield to the urge to view reality objectively. 'Colour and form alone cannot make up for the experience and excitement

160 OTTO DIX *Setting Sun in Winter Landscape* 1913

that are missing. I am deeply concerned to achieve an interpretation of our age in my pictures, for I believe a picture must first and foremost express a meaning, a theme', Dix later declared, thereby justifying his move towards realism. In 1919 Dix returned to his studies in Dresden and in 1922 went to the Düsseldorf art academy. In Dresden he was one of the founders of Gruppe 1919, whose programme was 'to take leave of old ways and old means once and for all, and then, working together and safeguarding the freedom of the personality, to seek and to find a new form of expression for that freedom and for the new world in which we live'. In Düsseldorf Dix joined Das junge Rheinland ('Young Rhineland'), which had also been founded in 1919.

New groups of artists were formed after the war in almost every large city in Germany, inspired by Expressionist and revolutionary

161 OTTO DIX *Self-portrait as Mars* 1915

fervour. The Novembergruppe, formed in Berlin in 1918, with Pechstein playing an important role in its foundation, aspired to a union of all German artists. Its first manifesto of 1918 stated: 'The future of art and the seriousness of this present time compel us, revolutionaries of the spirit (Expressionists, Cubists, Futurists), to the closest unity and agreement.' But their motto, 'Liberty, Equality, Fraternity', was not a programme that could be translated into politically relevant action. Although some of the members also belonged both to the Berliner Arbeitsrat für Kunst (Berlin Workers' Soviet for Art) and the Bauhaus, it did not prove possible to achieve organizational co-operation even between these two groups. The Bauhaus was the only body that managed to realize anything of its programme in practical terms. The Berliner Arbeitsrat für Kunst dissolved itself in 1921. The Novembergruppe degenerated into a pressure group, and politically engaged artists formed new groups such as the Kommune (Commune), the Bund revolutionärer Künstler (League of revolutionary artists) and, in 1924 the Rote Gruppe (Red Group), an association of Communist artists led by George Grosz.

It very quickly became apparent, however, that the Expressionist ideal of integration, held by the Brücke and the Blauer Reiter, and which Nolde had hoped for from the Neue Sezession, namely the idea of encouraging artists to abandon their isolation in favour of concerted effort, no longer had any force left in it. It was exhausted in manifestos, while other manifestos were simultaneously pouring scorn on Expressionism and proclaiming its imminent death. The Dadaist manifesto of 1918 declared bluntly: 'Expressionism . . . no longer has anything to do with the efforts made by active people.' And Yvan Goll, one of the few poets who had specifically declared themselves Expressionists, wrote with bitter contempt in 1921:

> If one wanted to be critical, it could certainly be proved that Expressionism is at its last gasp, thanks to the revolutionary carrion to which it tried to act the maternal Pythia. . . . And this is explained by the fact that the whole of Expressionism (1910–20) was not an artistic form but an attitude of mind. . . . Challenge. Manifesto. Appeal. Accusation. Oathtaking. Ecstasy. Battle. Mankind cries out. We are. One another. Passion . . . yes, yes, my dear brother Expressionist: taking life too seriously is the great danger today.

Giving a free rein to feeling looked like sentimentality when placed beside the fact that war and revolution had ended in apathy and the

162 LOVIS CORINTH
Self-portrait 1924

restoration of the previous order, instead of laying the foundations of a new world. In the growing consciousness of impotence, passion sounded like mockery, and became an empty, ineffective gesture; artistic forms degenerated into interesting calligraphy.

The Expressionists' slogan, 'Man is good', was replaced by its antithesis. George Grosz declared: 'Man is a beast'. The excitement and enthusiasm of the ego could no longer stand at the centre of things. It was replaced by the need to take a clear look at the banal and the mundane, to represent objects, in all their details, precisely and unsentimentally. As early as 1922 an inquiry was opened in *Das Kunstblatt* under the title 'A New Naturalism?', and in 1923 preparations began in Mannheim for an exhibition which was intended to show the work of artists 'who have remained, or have become once more, faithful to positive, tangible reality, with a confessional commitment'. The exhibition took place in 1925 with the title 'Neue Sachlichkeit' ('New Objectivity'), and this became the slogan of a new generation.

Bibliography

Books on individual artists are listed below in the Biographies section. Some useful general works:

Lothar-Günther Buchheim, *Die KG Brücke*, Feldafing 1956; *Der blaue Reiter*, Feldafing 1959.
Werner Haftmann, *Painting in the*

Twentieth Century, 2 vols, new edn, London New York 1965.
Klaus Lankheit (ed.), *The Blaue Reiter Almanac*, London and New York 1972.
Bernard S. Myers, *The German Expressionists*, New York 1957; British edn, *Expressionism*, London 1957.

F. & J. Roh, *German Art in the 20th Century*, London and Greenwich 1968
Peter Selz, *German Expressionist Painting*, Berkeley and Los Angeles 1957.
Paul Vogt, *Geschichte der deutschen Malerei im 20. Jrh.*, Cologne 1972.
John Willett, *Expressionism*, London and New York 1970.

Biographies

BARLACH, ERNST
Born 2 January 1870, Wedel (Holstein). Studied: 1888–91 at the Gewerbeschule, Hamburg; 1891–95 at the academy in Dresden, prize pupil of Robert Diez. 1895–96 first visit to Paris, studied at the Académie Julian. 1897 second visit to Paris, 1897–99 in Hamburg, first-prize winner in the competition for the design of the square outside the Rathaus in Hamburg. 1899–1901 resident in Berlin, 1901–04 in Wedel. 1904–05 taught at the school of ceramics in Höhr (Westerwald). 1905–10 resident in Berlin. 1906 journey to Russia. 1909 stayed in the Villa Romana in Florence, friendship with Theodor Däubler. 1910 moved to Güstrow (Mecklenburg). 1919 member of the Prussian Academy of Artists. 1924 Kleist Prize for his dramatic works. 1933 member of the order Pour le mérite; at the same time the first instances of his sculpture being removed from churches. 1937, 381 works confiscated as 'degenerate'. Died 24 October 1938 in Rostock.

BIBLIOGRAPHY: F. Schult, *Ernst Barlach. Das plastische Werk*, Hamburg 1960; F. Schult, *Ernst Barlach. Das graphische Werk*, Hamburg 1958; W. Stubbe, *Ernst Barlach. Zeichnungen*, Munich 1961.

BECKMANN, MAX
Born 12 February 1884, Leipzig. Educated in Brunswick, then, in 1899, started at the academy in Weimar under Carl Frithjof Smith. 1903 first visit to Paris. 1904 visits to Geneva and Florence, moved to Berlin. 1906 member of the Berlin Secession, Villa Romana prize with a bursary for a six-month stay in Florence. 1910 became a member of the committee of the Berlin Secession. 1914 volunteered for the medical corps, 1915 released from service after a nervous breakdown. Moved to Frankfurt am Main. 1925

Tutor at the Städelsches Kunstinstitut in Frankfurt. Further visits to Paris and Italy. 1933 dismissed from his teaching post, moved to Berlin. 1937 emigrated to Amsterdam, where he remained until 1947. 1947 appointment to Washington University, Saint Louis, Mo. 1949 appointment at the Art School of the Brooklyn Museum, New York. Died 27 December 1950 in New York.

BIBLIOGRAPHY: G. Busch, *Max Beckmann*, Munich 1960; B. Reifenberg and W. Hausenstein, *Max Beckmann*, Munich 1949; L. G. Buchheim, *Max Beckmann*, Feldafing 1959. P. Selz, *Max Beckmann*, New York 1964.

CAMPENDONK, HEINRICH
Born 3 November 1889, Krefeld. 1905 studied at the Kunstgewerbeschule in Krefeld under Johan Thorn-Prikker. 1911 moved to Sindelsdorf in Upper Bavaria on the suggestion of Marc. From then on a member of the Blauer Reiter circle, with whom he exhibited. 1914–16 military service. 1922 appointment as a teacher at the Kunstschule in Essen, 1923 to Krefeld and 1926 to the academy in Düsseldorf. 1933 removed from teaching post. After a stay in Belgium, moved to Amsterdam, where he was appointed to the Rijksakademie. Died 1957 in Amsterdam.

BIBLIOGRAPHY: P. Wember, *Heinrich Campendonk*, Krefeld 1960.

CORINTH, LOVIS
Born 21 July 1858, Tapiau (East Prussia). Studied: 1876 at the Kunstakademie in Königsberg, 1880 at the Munich academy, 1884 in Antwerp and then the Académie Julian in Paris. Moved between Paris, Berlin and Königsberg. Settled in Munich in 1891. 1900 visit to Denmark. 1901 moved to Berlin and opened his own school. 1911 elected chairman of the Berlin Secession. Up to the outbreak of war in 1914 many

visits to France and Italy. 1915 appointed president of the Berlin Secession. 1919 built a house on the Walchensee (Upper Bavaria) where he painted numerous landscapes in the remaining years of his life. Died 17 July 1925 during a visit to Zandvoort in Holland.

BIBLIOGRAPHY: C. Berend-Corinth, *Die Gemälde von Lovis Corinth*, Munich 1958; G. von der Osten, *Lovis Corinth*, Munich 1950; *Lovis Corinth*, cat., Tate Gallery, London 1959.

DIX, OTTO
Born 2 December 1891, Untermhaus bei Gera. 1905–09 studied painting. 1909–14 studied at the Kunstgewerbeschule in Dresden. 1914–18 military service. 1919–21 studied at the academy in Dresden. 1919 co-founder of Gruppe 1919. 1922–25 prize scholar at the Düsseldorf academy, member of Das junge Rheinland. 1925–27 resident in Berlin. 1927 appointed to the staff of the Dresden academy. 1933 dismissed from teaching post. 1934 banned from exhibiting. 1935 moved to Hemmenhofen on Lake Constance. 1939 arrested by the Gestapo on suspicion of being involved in the Munich assassination attempt. 1945–46 interned by the French. Died 25 July 1969 at Singen.

BIBLIOGRAPHY: F. Löffler, *Otto Dix*, Dresden 1960.

FEININGER, LYONEL
Born 17 July 1871, New York. 1887 moved to Europe and began studying at the Kunstgewerbeschule in Hamburg. 1888 moved to Berlin. Began drawing caricatures for *Humoristische Blätter*. 1891 resumed study at the Berlin academy. 1892–93 stayed in Paris, studying in Colarossi's studio. 1906–08 second stay in Paris, again working in Colarossi's studio. 1908 moved again to Berlin. 1909 gave up working as a cartoonist and took up

painting in earnest. 1911 showed six pictures at the Salon des Indépendants in Paris. 1912 friendship with Kubin, Heckel and Schmidt-Rottluff. 1919 appointed to the staff of the Bauhaus in Weimar. 1926 moved to Dessau with the Bauhaus. 1933 moved to Berlin. 1936 short stay in the United States, where he returned in 1937 to stay for good. From 1938 resident in New York. Died 13 January 1956 in New York.

BIBLIOGRAPHY: Hans Hess, *Lyonel Feininger*, London and New York 1961.

HECKEL, ERICH

Born 31 July 1883, Döbeln (Saxony). Up to 1904 attended the Gymnasium (high school) in Chemnitz, friendship with fellow-pupil Karl Schmidt-Rottluff dating from 1901. 1904–05 studied architecture at the Technische Hochschule in Dresden. Friendship with Ernst Ludwig Kirchner and Fritz Bleyl. 1905 co-founder of the Brücke group. 1906 met Max Pechstein and Emil Nolde. 1910 friendship with Otto Mueller, co-founder of the Neue Sezession in Berlin. 1911 moved to Berlin. 1913 dissolution of the Brücke. 1915–18 voluntary service with the Red Cross in Flanders, where he met Max Beckmann and James Ensor. From 1924 frequent journeys about Europe. 1937 confiscation of 729 works. 1944 destruction of his Berlin studio, moved to Hemmenhofen on Lake Constance. 1949 appointed to the Karlsruhe academy, worked there until 1955. Died 27 January 1970 in Hemmenhofen.

BIBLIOGRAPHY: P. Vogt, *Erich Heckel*, Recklinghausen 1965; A. and W.-D. Dube, *Erich Heckel, Das graphische Werk*, 2 vols, New York 1964–65.

JAWLENSKY, ALEXEJ VON

Born 13 March 1864 in Torzhok (Gouvernement Tver). From 1882 attended the military academy in Moscow. 1889 transferred to St Petersburg. Attended the academy of art there as well as performing military duties. 1891 met Marianne Werefkin. 1896 resigned his commission and went to Munich with Marianne Werefkin. 1896–99 at Anton Azbé's school of art, where he met Kandinsky in 1897. 1905 visited France, where he exhibited in the Salon d'Automne. 1908 spent the summer in Murnau with Kandinsky, Münter and Werefkin. 1909 co-founder of the Neue Künstlervereinigung München. 1911 visited Paris, met Matisse. 1912 met Klee and Nolde, break-up of the Neue Künstlervereinigung. 1914 moved to Switzerland on

the outbreak of war. 1921 moved to Wiesbaden. Died 15 March 1941 in Wiesbaden.

BIBLIOGRAPHY: C. Weiler, *Alexej Jawlensky*, Cologne 1959.

KANDINSKY, WASSILY

Born 4 December 1866 in Moscow. From 1886 studied jurisprudence and political economy. 1892 qualified as a lawyer. 1895 refused an appointment at the university of Tartu and instead moved to Munich, in order to become a painter. 1897–99 studied at Anton Azbé's school of art, where he met Jawlensky. 1900 studied under Stuck at the Munich academy. 1901 co-founder of the Phalanx association of artists. 1902 met Gabriele Münter. 1903–08 travelled about Europe. Exhibited in Paris at the Salon d'Automne and the Salon des Indépendants during these years. From 1908 again resident in Munich, spending the summer in Murnau with Jawlensky, Münter and Werefkin. 1909 co-founder and chairman of the Neue Künstlervereinigung. 1910 friendship with Franz Marc. Wrote *Über das Geistige in der Kunst*. 1911 left the Neue Künstlervereinigung, collaborated with Marc on the Blauer Reiter almanac and organized the first exhibition under the same name. 1914 moved to Switzerland on the outbreak of war, and later returned to Moscow. 1918 member of the Commissariat for Popular Enlightenment, tutor at the Moscow university. 1920 tutor at Moscow university. 1921 moved to Berlin. From 1922 teacher at the Bauhaus in Weimar. 1933 moved to Paris. 1937 declared 'degenerate'. Died 13 December 1944 at Neuilly-sur-Seine.

BIBLIOGRAPHY: W. Grohmann, *Kandinsky*, New York 1960.

KIRCHNER, ERNST LUDWIG

Born 6 May 1880, Aschaffenburg. From 1890 resident in Chemnitz. 1901 began to study architecture at the Technische Hochschule in Dresden. 1902 friendship with Fritz Bleyl. 1903 two semesters at the school of Debschitz and Obrist in Munich. 1904 return to Dresden, friendship with Erich Heckel. 1905 qualified as an engineer at the Technische Hochschule and took up painting full time. Friendship with Karl Schmidt-Rottluff. Co-founder of the Brücke group. 1906 met Nolde and Pechstein. 1908 spent the summer on Fehmarn for the first time. 1910 co-founder of the Neue Sezession in Berlin. Friendship with

Otto Mueller. 1911 visit to Bohemia with Mueller. Moved to Berlin. 1913 break-up of the Brücke. 1914–15 military service, released after physical and mental breakdown. 1917 moved to Davos. Remained in Frauenkirch near Davos after his recovery. 1937, 639 works confiscated as 'degenerate'. Committed suicide 15 June 1938 in Frauenkirch.

BIBLIOGRAPHY: D. E. Gordon, *Ernst Ludwig Kirchner*, Munich 1968 (includes a complete catalogue of the works); A. and W.-D. Dube, *E.L. Kirchner, Das graphische Werk*, Munich 1967. W. Grohmann, *E.L. Kirchner*, London and New York 1961.

KLEE, PAUL

Born 18 December 1879, München-buchsee near Berne. 1898 began studying painting with Heinrich Knirr in Munich, 1900 joined Stuck's class at the Munich academy. 1901–02 visits to Italy. 1905 visited Paris. 1906 moved to Munich. 1910 first major exhibition in Switzerland. Friendship with Kubin. 1911 met the members of the Blauer Reiter circle. 1912 visited Paris, met Delaunay. 1914 co-founder of the Munich Neue Sezession. 1916–18 military service. 1920 appointed to the staff of the Bauhaus in Weimar. 1931 appointment at the Düsseldorf academy. 1933 moved to Berne. 1937 declared 'degenerate' in Germany. Died 29 June 1940 at Locarno-Muralto.

BIBLIOGRAPHY: W. Grohmann, *Paul Klee*, London and New York 1967; W. Haftmann, *The Mind and Work of Paul Klee*, London and New York 1954.

KOKOSCHKA, OSKAR

Born 1 March 1886, Pöchlarn. 1905–09 student at the Kunstgewerbeschule in Vienna, with the intention of becoming a teacher. 1907–09 worked with the Wiener Werkstätte. 1910 moved to Berlin, worked on *Der Sturm*. First collective exhibition in Berlin. 1911 returned to Vienna, assistant tutor at the Kunstgewerbeschule. 1912 exhibited with the Blauer Reiter in Berlin. 1913 visit to Italy. 1914–15 military service, terminated by severe injury. 1917 shorter periods of residence in Dresden and Stockholm, then settled in Dresden until 1924. 1919 appointed to the staff of the Dresden academy. 1924 resigned post. Travelled in Switzerland and in Italy and France. 1925–33 travels in Europe and North Africa, with Paris as his base. 1934–38 resident in Prague. 1937, 417 works confiscated in Germany. 1938 fled to London. Took up permanent residence in London from 1940. 1947 British citizenship. 1953 moved to Villeneuve on Lake Geneva. Foundation of the International Summer School for visual arts in Salzburg. Died 22 February 1980 at Montreux.

BIBLIOGRAPHY: H. M. Wingler, *Oskar Kokoschka – The Works of the Painter*, Salzburg 1956; E. Hoffmann, *Kokoschka – Life and Work*, London 1947.

KUBIN, ALFRED
Born 10 April 1877, Leitmeritz (now Litoměřice in Czechoslovakia). 1891–92 student at the Kunstgewerbeschule in Salzburg. 1892–96 apprenticed to a photographer in Klagenfurt. 1897 military service. 1898–1901 studied at Schmidt-Reutte's school of art and under Gysis at the academy in Munich. 1902 first exhibition in Berlin. 1905–06 travelled in France and Italy. 1909 travelled in the Balkans. Friendship with members of the Neue Künstlervereinigung in Munich. 1912 exhibited with the Blauer Reiter. 1914 visit to Paris. 1924 stay in Switzerland. 1930 member of the Prussian academy of arts. Died 20 August 1959 at Zwickledt.

BIBLIOGRAPHY: P. Raabe, *Alfred Kubin. Leben, Werk, Wirkung*, Hamburg 1957.

MACKE, AUGUST
Born 3 January 1887, Meschede (Sauerland). 1904–06 student at the academy and Kunstgewerbeschule in Düsseldorf. 1905 designs for stage sets and costumes for Düsseldorf theatre. Travelled to Italy. 1906 travelled to Holland and London. 1907 travelled to Paris. Studied under Corinth in Berlin. 1908 travelled to Italy and Paris. 1909 travelled to Paris, moved to the Tegernsee. 1910 friendship with Franz Marc. Contacts with the Neue Künstlervereinigung in Munich. Moved to Bonn. 1911 collaborated on the Blauer Reiter almanac. 1912 visited Paris with Marc. 1913 stayed on the lake of Thun. 1914 visited Tunis with Moilliet and Klee. Killed 26 September 1914 at Perthesles-Hurlus, Champagne.

BIBLIOGRAPHY: G. Vries, *August Macke*, 2nd edn, Stuttgart 1957; M. S. Fox (ed.), *August Macke. Tunisian Watercolors and Drawings*, New York 1959.

MARC, FRANZ
Born 8 February 1880, Munich. After initially studying theology, 1900–03 studied under Hackel and Diez at the Munich academy. 1902 visited Italy. 1903 visited France. 1906 visit to Greece. 1907 visit to Paris. 1909 moved to Sindelsdorf (Upper Bavaria). 1910 friendship with August Macke. Contacts with the Neue Künstlervereinigung in Munich. Friendship with Kandinsky. 1911 member and later third president of the Neue Künstlervereinigung, Munich. With Kandinsky, organized the first Blauer Reiter exhibition. 1912 visited Paris with Macke. The almanac *Der Blaue Reiter*, edited by Marc and Kandinsky, published in Munich. 1914 moved to Ried (Upper Bavaria). Called up for military service. Killed 4 March 1916 at Verdun.

BIBLIOGRAPHY: K. Lankheit, *Franz Marc. Katalog der Werke*, Cologne 1970; A. J. Schardt, *Franz Marc*, Berlin 1936; K. Lankheit, *Franz Marc. Watercolors, Drawings, Writings*, London and New York 1960.

MEIDNER, LUDWIG
Born 18 April 1884, Bernstadt (Silesia). 1901–02 builder's apprentice. 1903–05 student at the academy in Breslau. 1905–06 fashion artist in Berlin. 1906–07 stayed in Paris; friendship with Modigliani. 1908 returned to Berlin. 1912 co-founder of Die Pathetiker. 1916–18 military service. 1924–25 tutor at the *Studienateliers* (study workshops) for painting and sculpture in Berlin. 1935 moved to Cologne. Drawing master at the Jewish high school. 1939 fled to England. 1952 returned to Germany. Died 14 May 1966 in Darmstadt.

BIBLIOGRAPHY: T. Grochowiak, *Ludwig Meidner*, Recklinghausen 1966.

MORGNER, WILHELM
Born 27 January 1891, Soest (Westphalia). 1908 pupil of Georg Tappert at Worpswede. 1910 stayed in Berlin. 1912 worked on *Der Sturm*. 1913 called up for military service. Killed at Langemark, August 1917.

MUELLER, OTTO
Born 16 October 1874, Liebau (in the Riesengebirge, Saxony). 1890–94 studied lithography in Görlitz. 1894–96 student at the Dresden academy. 1896–97 travelled in Switzerland and Italy with Gerhart Hauptmann. 1898–99 stayed in Munich. 1899 returned to Dresden. 1908 moved to Berlin. Friendship with Lehmbruck. 1910 met the members of the Brücke. Joined the Brücke and the Neue Sezession in Berlin. 1911 visited Bohemia with Kirchner. 1916–18 military service. 1919 appointed to the staff of the academy in Breslau. 1924–30 travelled in the Balkans. Died 24 Sept 1930 in Breslau.

BIBLIOGRAPHY: L. G. Buchheim, *Otto Mueller. Leben und Werk*, Feldafing 1963.

MÜNTER, GABRIELE
Born 19 February 1877 in Berlin. 1897 studied art in Düsseldorf. 1901 student at the school of the Künstlerinnenverein in Munich. 1902 studied under Kandinsky at the Phalanx school. 1904–08 travelled with Kandinsky. 1908 working holiday at Murnau with Kandinsky, Jawlensky and Werefkin. 1909 co-founder of the Neue Künstlervereinigung. 1911 co-founder of the Blauer Reiter. 1914 separation from Kandinsky. 1916–20 travelled in Scandinavia. 1925–29 resident in Berlin. 1931 moved to Murnau. Died 19 May 1962 at Murnau.

BIBLIOGRAPHY: J. Eichner, *Kandinsky und Gabriele Münter*, Munich 1957.

NAUEN, HEINRICH
Born 1 June 1880 in Krefeld. 1898 student at the Düsseldorf academy. 1899–1902 student at the Stuttgart academy. 1902–05 resident in Belgium. 1906–11 resident in Berlin. 1911 moved to Dilborn. 1915–18 military service. 1921 appointed to the staff of the Düsseldorf academy. 1931 moved to Neuss. 1937 dismissed from teaching post. 1938 moved to Kalkar. Died 26 November 1940 at Kalkar.

BIBLIOGRAPHY: E. Marx, *Heinrich Nauen*, Recklinghausen 1966.

NOLDE, EMIL (EMIL HANSEN)
Born 7 August 1867, Nolde. 1884–88 attended the Sauerman school of carving in Flensburg. 1892–98 teacher at the Kunstgewerbeschule at St Gall (Switzerland). 1900 visited Paris. 1901 moved to Berlin. From 1903 spent the summers on the island of Alsen. 1905 visited Italy. 1906–07 member of the Brücke. 1910 expelled from the Berlin Sezession, co-founder of the Neue Sezession. 1913–14 took part in an Imperial Colonial Office expedition to New Guinea. From 1917 spent the summers in Utewarf. 1921 visited England, Spain and France. 1927 moved to Seebüll. 1931 member of the Prussian Academy of Arts. 1937, 1052 works confiscated. 1941 forbidden to paint. Died 13 April 1956 at Seebüll.

BIBLIOGRAPHY: G. Schiefler, *Emil Nolde, Das graphische Werk*, ed. C. Mosel. 2 vols, Cologne 1966–67; M. Sauerlandt, *Emil Nolde*, Munich 1921; W. Haftmann, *Emil Nolde*, London and New York 1959.

PECHSTEIN, MAX
Born 31 December 1881, Eckersbach, near Zwickau. 1896–1900 apprenticed to a decorator. 1900–02 student at the Kunstgewerbeschule in Dresden. 1902–06 student at the Dresden academy. 1906 member of the Brücke. 1907–08 stayed in Italy. 1908 stayed in Paris. Moved to Berlin. From 1909 spent the summers on the Kurische Nehrung. 1910 co-founder and chairman of the Neue Sezession in Berlin. 1911, 1913 visits to Italy. 1914–15 travelled to the Palau Islands in the South Pacific. 1916–18 military service. 1918 co-founder and chairman of the Novembergruppe. 1922 member of the Prussian Academy. 1934 expelled from the academy and the Berlin Secession. 1940 moved to Pomerania. 1945 returned to Berlin. Appointed to the staff of the Hochschule für bildende Künste in Berlin. Died 29 June 1955 in Berlin.

BIBLIOGRAPHY: P. Fechter, *Das graphische Werk Max Pechsteins*, Berlin 1921; M. Osborn, *Max Pechstein*, Berlin 1922.

ROHLFS, CHRISTIAN
Born 22 December 1849, Niendorf (Holstein). 1870 began his studies at the academy in Weimar. 1884 completed studies, free studio at the academy. 1895 moved to Berlin. 1901 moved to Hagen. 1910–11 resident in and near Munich. Member of the Neue Sezession in Berlin. 1924 member of the Prussian Academy of Arts. 1927 first visit to Ascona. 1937 declared 'degenerate'; expelled from the Prussian Academy; banned from exhibiting. Died 8 January 1938 at Hagen.

BIBLIOGRAPHY: P. Vogt, *Christian Rohlfs. Das graphische Werk*, Recklinghausen n.d.; W. Scheidig, *Christian Rohlfs*, Dresden 1965.

SCHIELE, EGON
Born 12 June 1890, Tulln. 1906 began studying at the academy in Vienna. 1909 completed studies. Co-founder of the Neukunstgruppe. 1911 moved to Krumau in Bohemia. 1912 returned to Vienna. Imprisoned for producing pornographic drawings. 1915 conscripted. Died 31 October 1918.

BIBLIOGRAPHY: O. Kallir, *Egon Schiele*, Vienna 1966.

SCHMIDT-ROTTLUFF, KARL
Born 1 December 1884, Rottluff (Saxony). Attended school in Chemnitz. 1905 began to study architecture in Dresden. Co-founder of the Brücke. 1907–12 spent the summers at Dangast. 1911 visited Norway. Moved to Berlin. 1915–18 military service. Until 1931 spent the summers in Pomerania. 1923 visited Italy. 1924 visited Paris. 1931 member of the Prussian Academy of Arts. 1938 more than 600 works confiscated. 1941 forbidden to paint. 1947 appointed to the staff of the Hochschule für bildende Künste in Berlin. Died 1976.

BIBLIOGRAPHY: W. Grohmann, *Karl Schmidt-Rottluff*, Stuttgart 1956.

List of Illustrations

The medium is oil on canvas unless specified; measurements are given in inches and centimetres, height before width.

BARLACH, ERNST (1870–1938)
135 *Couple in Conversation*, 1912. Lithograph, $10\frac{3}{8} \times 13\frac{3}{8}$ (26·3 × 34). 136 *The Cathedrals*, 1922. Woodcut, $10 \times 14\frac{1}{8}$ (25·5 × 36).

BECHTEJEFF, WLADIMIR VON
75 *Horse-trainer, c.* 1912. $43\frac{1}{4} \times 37$ (110 × 94). Städtische Galerie, Munich.

BECKMANN, MAX (1884–1950)
124 *Large Deathbed Scene*, 1906. $51\frac{1}{8} \times 55\frac{7}{8}$ (130 × 142). G. Franke collection, Munich. 125 *Deposition*, 1917. $59\frac{1}{2} \times 50\frac{3}{4}$ (151 × 129). The Museum of Modern Art, New York. 126 *The Night*, 1918. $52\frac{3}{4} \times 61\frac{1}{2}$ (134 × 156). Kunstsammlung Nordrhein-Westfalen, Düsseldorf. 127 *The Synagogue*, 1919. $35 \times 55\frac{1}{4}$ (89 × 140·5). Private collection. 128 *Before the Masked Ball*, 1922. $31\frac{1}{2} \times 51\frac{1}{4}$ (80 × 130). Staatsgalerie moderner Kunst, Munich. 129 *Self-portrait with a Red Scarf*, 1917. $31\frac{1}{2} \times 23\frac{5}{8}$ (80 × 60). Staatsgalerie, Stuttgart. 130 *Carnival*, 1920. $73\frac{1}{4} \times 36\frac{1}{4}$ (186 × 92). Private collection, Hamburg.

CAMPENDONK, HEINRICH (1889–1957)
119 *Leaping Horse*, 1911. $33\frac{1}{2} \times 25\frac{5}{8}$ (85 × 65). Saarlandmuseum, Saarbrücken. 120 *Girl Playing a Shawm*, 1914. $21\frac{1}{4} \times 12\frac{5}{8}$ (54 × 32). Städt. Galerie, Munich.

CORINTH, LOVIS (1858–1925)
159 *The Red Christ*, 1922. Oil on panel, $53\frac{1}{8} \times 42\frac{1}{8}$ (135 × 107). Staatsgalerie moderner Kunst, Munich. 162 *Self-portrait*, 1924. $54 \times 42\frac{1}{8}$ (137 × 107). Staatsgalerie moderner Kunst, Munich.

DIX, OTTO (1891–1969)
160 *Setting Sun in Winter Landscape*, 1913. Oil on cardboard, $20\frac{1}{8} \times 26$ (51 × 66). Private collection, Stuttgart. 161 *Self-portrait as Mars*, 1915. $31\frac{7}{8} \times 26$ (81 × 66). Haus der Heimat, Freital.

ERBSLÖH, ADOLF (1881–1947)
76 *Brannenburg (Sunset)*, 1911. Oil on cardboard, $15\frac{1}{8} \times 18\frac{7}{8}$ (38·5 × 48). O. Stangl collection, Munich. 78 *Nude with Garter*, 1909. $40\frac{1}{2} \times 29\frac{1}{2}$ (103 × 75). Staatsgalerie moderner Kunst, Munich.

FEININGER, LYONEL (1871–1956)
131 *Gelmeroda I*, 1913. $39\frac{3}{8} \times 31\frac{1}{2}$ (100 × 80). Stefan Pauson collection, Glasgow. 132 *Cycle Race*, 1912. $31\frac{1}{2} \times 39\frac{3}{8}$ (80 × 100). Lately on the art market. 133 *Zirchow V*, 1916. $31\frac{1}{2} \times 39\frac{3}{8}$ (80 × 100). The Brooklyn Museum, New York. 134 *Bathers II*, 1917. $33\frac{1}{2} \times 39\frac{3}{4}$ (85 × 101). Harry Fuld collection, London.

HECKEL, ERICH (1883–1970)
10 Poster for Brücke Exhibition, 1908. Woodcut, $33 \times 23\frac{1}{2}$ (84 × 59·6). 13 Invitation to Brücke Exhibition, 1912. Coloured woodcut, $3\frac{3}{4} \times 2\frac{7}{8}$ (9·6 × 7·2). 31 *Flowering Trees*, 1906. Woodcut, $4 \times 7\frac{1}{8}$ (10 × 18). 32 *Brickworks*, 1907. $26\frac{3}{4} \times 33\frac{5}{8}$ (68 × 86). Roman Norbert Ketterer collection, Campione. 33 *Village Dance*, 1908. $26\frac{3}{8} \times 29\frac{1}{8}$ (67 × 74). Nationalgalerie, Berlin. 34 *Woodland Pond*, 1910. $37\frac{3}{4} \times 47\frac{1}{4}$ (96 × 120). Staatsgalerie moderner Kunst, Munich (loan from L. G. Buchheim collection) 35 *At the Writing-desk*, 1911. Lithograph, $13 \times 10\frac{5}{8}$ (33 × 27). 36 *Nude on a Sofa*, 1909. $37\frac{3}{4} \times 47\frac{1}{4}$ (96 × 120). Staatsgalerie moderner Kunst, Munich. 37 *Glassy Day*, 1913. $47\frac{1}{4} \times 37\frac{3}{4}$ (120 × 96). Staatsgalerie moderner Kunst, Munich (loan from M. Kruss collection). 38 *Crouching Woman*, 1913. Woodcut, $16\frac{1}{2} \times 12\frac{1}{4}$ (42 × 31). 39 *Two Men at a Table*, 1912. $37\frac{3}{4} \times 47\frac{1}{4}$ (96 × 120). Kunsthalle, Hamburg. 40 *Man on a Plain*, 1917. Woodcut, $15 \times 10\frac{5}{8}$ (38 × 27). 41 *Madonna of Ostend*, 1915. Tempera on canvas, $118\frac{1}{8} \times 59$ (300 × 150). Destroyed. 42 *Portrait of a Man*, 1919. Coloured woodcut, $18\frac{1}{8} \times 13$ (46 × 33).

HOELZEL, ADOLF (1853–1934)
6 *Composition in Red*, 1905. $26\frac{3}{4} \times 33\frac{1}{2}$ (68 × 85). Günther Wagner collection, Hanover. 7 *Landscape*, *c.* 1905. $15\frac{3}{8} \times 19\frac{1}{4}$ (39 × 49). Staatsgalerie, Stuttgart.

JAWLENSKY, ALEXEJ VON (1864–1941)
87 *Yellow Houses*, 1909. Oil on cardboard, $21\frac{1}{4} \times 19\frac{3}{4}$ (54 × 50). O. Henkell collection, Wiesbaden. 88 *Still-life with Fruit*, *c.* 1910. Oil on cardboard, $18\frac{7}{8} \times 26\frac{3}{4}$ (48 × 68). Städtische Galerie, Munich. 89 *Solitude*, 1912. Oil on cardboard, $13 \times 17\frac{3}{4}$ (33 × 45). Museum am Ostwall, Dortmund. 90 *Spanish Girl with Black Shawl*, 1913. Oil on cardboard, $26\frac{3}{4} \times 18\frac{7}{8}$ (67 × 48). Städtische Galerie, Munich. 91 *Large Female Head*, 1917. Oil on cardboard, $19\frac{3}{4} \times 15\frac{3}{4}$ (50 × 40). Wilhelm-Lehmbruck-Museum, Duisburg. 92 *Divine Radiance*, 1918. Oil on cardboard, 17×13 (43 × 33). O. Stangl collection, Munich. 97 *Girl with Peonies*, 1909. Oil on cardboard, $39\frac{3}{4} \times 29\frac{1}{2}$ (101 × 75). Städtisches Museum, Wuppertal.

KANDINSKY, WASSILY (1866–1944)
72 Poster for the 1st Exhibition of the Neue Künstlervereinigung München, 1909. $10\frac{5}{8} \times 8\frac{1}{2}$ (27 × 21·5). 73 Membership card of the Neue Künstlervereinigung München, from the woodcut 'Cliffs', 1908–09. $5\frac{1}{2} \times 5\frac{5}{8}$ (14·1 × 14·4). 79 Title vignette for the catalogue of the 1st Exhibition of the Blaue Reiter, 1911. $2\frac{3}{8} \times 1\frac{3}{4}$ (6 × 4·5). 80 Cover of the *Almanach der Blaue Reiter*, 1911. Coloured woodcut, $11 \times 8\frac{1}{4}$ (28 × 21). 81 *Singer*, 1903. Coloured woodcut, $7\frac{7}{8} \times 5\frac{7}{8}$ (20 × 15). 82 *Beach Tents in Holland*, 1904. Oil on cardboard, $9\frac{1}{2} \times 12\frac{7}{8}$ (24 × 32·6). Städtische Galerie, Munich. 83 *Village Church*, 1908. Oil on cardboard, $13 \times 17\frac{3}{4}$ (33 × 45). Städtisches Museum, Wuppertal. 84 *Mountain Landscape with Church*, 1910. Oil on cardboard, $13 \times 17\frac{3}{4}$ (33 × 45). Städtische Galerie, Munich. 85 *Mountain*, 1909. $42\frac{7}{8} \times 42\frac{7}{8}$ (109 × 109). Städtische Galerie, Munich. 86 *Improvisation No. 19*, 1911. $47\frac{1}{4} \times 55\frac{3}{4}$ (120 · 141·5). Städtische Galerie, Munich. 95 *Landscape with Tower*, 1909. Oil on cardboard, $29\frac{1}{2} \times 39\frac{1}{4}$ (75·5 × 99·5). Nina Kandinsky collection, Paris. 98 *With a Black Arc*, 1912. $74 \times 77\frac{1}{8}$ (188 × 196). Nina Kandinsky collection, Paris. 99 *Dreamy Improvisation*, 1913. $51\frac{1}{4} \times 51\frac{1}{4}$ (130 × 130). Staatsgalerie moderner Kunst, Munich.

KANOLDT, ALEXANDER (1881–1939)
77 *At the Eisack*, 1911. $25\frac{3}{4} \times 31\frac{3}{4}$ (65·5 × 81·5). O. Stangl collection, Munich.

KIRCHNER, ERNST LUDWIG (1880–1938)
11 Cover of 4th annual portfolio of the Brücke, 1909. Woodcut, $15\frac{1}{2} \times 11$ (39·5 × 27·9). 14 Title woodcut of catalogue of Brücke Exhibition, Berlin and Hamburg, 1912. 15 Title woodcut of *Chronik der Künstlergruppe Brücke*, 1913. 18×13 (45·7 × 33·2). 16 *A Group of Artists*, 1926. $66\frac{1}{8} \times 49\frac{5}{8}$ (168 × 126). Wallraf-Richartz Museum, Cologne. 17 *Lake in the Park*, 1906. Oil on cardboard, $20\frac{1}{2} \times 27\frac{1}{2}$ (52 × 70). E. Teltsch collection, London. 18 *Three Bathers by the Moritzburg Lakes*, 1909. Etching, 7×8 (17·8 × 20·5). 19 *Tramlines in Dresden*, 1909. $27\frac{1}{2} \times 30\frac{7}{8}$ (70 × 78·5). Dr Fischer collection, Stuttgart. 20 *Rumanian Artiste*, 1910. Lithograph, $12\frac{3}{4} \times 15$ (32·5 × 38). 21 *Bareback Rider*, 1912. $47\frac{1}{4} \times 39\frac{3}{8}$ (120 × 100). Roman Norbert Ketterer collection, Campione. 22 *Street by Schöneberg Municipal Park*, 1913. $47\frac{1}{4} \times 59$ (120 × 150). Harry Lynde Bradley collection, Milwaukee. 23 *Women at Potsdamer Platz*, 1914. Woodcut, $20\frac{1}{8} \times 14\frac{1}{2}$ (51 × 37). 24 *Figures Walking into the Sea*, 1912. $57\frac{1}{2} \times 78\frac{3}{4}$ (146 × 200). Staatsgalerie, Stuttgart. 25 *Peter Schlemihl: Conflict*, 1915. Coloured woodcut, $13\frac{1}{8} \times 8\frac{1}{4}$ (33·5 × 21). 26 *Ludwig Schames*, 1918. Woodcut, $22 \times 9\frac{7}{8}$ (56 × 25). 27 *The Drinker (Self-portrait)*, 1915. $46\frac{1}{2} \times 34\frac{5}{8}$ (118 × 88). Germanisches Nationalmuseum, Nuremberg. 28 *Semi-nude Woman with Hat*, 1911. $29\frac{7}{8} \times 27\frac{1}{2}$ (76 × 70). Wallraf-Richartz Museum, Cologne. 29 *Five Women in the Street*, 1913. $47\frac{1}{4} \times 35\frac{1}{2}$ (120 × 90). Wallraf-Richartz Museum, Cologne. 30 *Moonlit Winter Night*, 1919. $47\frac{1}{4} \times 47\frac{5}{8}$ (120 × 121). Institute of Arts, Detroit.

KLEE, PAUL (1879–1940)
114 *The Föhn Wind in the Marcs' Garden*, 1915. Watercolour, $7\frac{7}{8} \times 5\frac{7}{8}$ (20 × 15). Städtische Galerie, Munich. 117 *Scene in Restaurant*, 1911. Pen and ink drawing, $5\frac{1}{8} \times 9$ (13 × 23). Felix Klee collection, Berne. 118 *In the Houses of Saint-Germain (Tunis)*, 1914. Watercolour, $6\frac{1}{8} \times 6\frac{1}{4}$ (15·5 × 16). Felix Klee collection, Berne.

KLINGER, MAX (1857–1920)
3 *Christ on Olympus*. Museum der bildenden Künste, Leipzig.

KOKOSCHKA, OSKAR (1886–1980)
123 Poster design for *Der Sturm*, *c.* 1910. Museum of Fine Arts, Budapest. 139 *Still-life with Pineapple*, 1907. $43\frac{3}{8} \times 31\frac{1}{8}$ (110 × 80). Nationalgalerie, Berlin. 140 Drawing for *Mörder Hoffnung der Frauen*, *c.* 1908. $8\frac{1}{2} \times 6\frac{7}{8}$ (21·6 × 17·5). Staatsgalerie, Stuttgart. 141 *Auguste*

Forel, *c.* 1909. $28 \times 22\frac{7}{8}$ (71 × 58). Städtische Kunsthalle, Mannheim. 142 *Herwarth Walden*, 1910. $39\frac{3}{8} \times 26\frac{3}{4}$ (100 × 68). Staatsgalerie, Stuttgart. 143 *The Temptation of Christ*, 1911–12. $31\frac{1}{2} \times 50$ (80 × 127). Osterreichische Galerie, Vienna. 144 *Landscape in the Dolomites: Tre Croci*, 1913. $32\frac{1}{4} \times 46\frac{7}{8}$ (82 × 119). Private collection, Hamburg. 145 *The Bride of the Wind (The Tempest)*, 1914. $71\frac{1}{4} \times 86\frac{5}{8}$ (181 × 220). Kunstmuseum, Basle. 146 *The Emigrés*, 1916–17. $37 \times 57\frac{1}{8}$ (94 × 145). Staatsgalerie moderner Kunst, Munich. 147 *Woman in Blue*, *c.* 1919. $29\frac{1}{2} \times 39\frac{3}{8}$ (75 × 100). Staatsgalerie, Stuttgart. 148 *Neustadt, Dresden*, *c.* 1922. $31\frac{1}{2} \times 47\frac{1}{4}$ (80 × 120). Kunsthalle, Hamburg.

KUBIN, ALFRED (1877–1959)
121 Drawing from the *Almanach der Blaue Reiter*, 1911. Pen and ink. 122 Drawing from the *Almanach der Blaue Reiter*, 1911. Pen and ink.

LEISTIKOW, WALTER (1865–1908)
5 *Danish Landscape*. $31\frac{1}{2} \times 39\frac{3}{8}$ (80 × 100). Kunsthistorisches Museum, Vienna.

LIEBERMANN, MAX (1847–1935)
2 *Parrot Walk, Amsterdam Zoo*, 1902. $34\frac{5}{8} \times 28\frac{3}{8}$ (88 × 72). Kunsthalle, Bremen.

MACKE, AUGUST (1887–1914)
1 *Girls Bathing*, 1913. $39\frac{3}{8} \times 31\frac{1}{2}$ (100 × 80). Staatsgalerie moderner Kunst, Munich. 109 *Girls Among Trees*, 1914. $47 \times 62\frac{5}{8}$ (119·5 × 159). Staatsgalerie moderner Kunst, Munich. 110 *Lady in a Green Jacket*, 1913. $17\frac{1}{2} \times 17\frac{1}{8}$ (44·5 × 43·5). Wallraf-Richartz Museum, Cologne. 111 *Zoological Garden I*, 1912. $23 \times 38\frac{5}{8}$ (58·5 × 98). Städtische Galerie, Munich. 112 *Large, Well-lit Shop Window*, 1912. $41\frac{3}{8} \times 33\frac{1}{2}$ (105 × 85). Landesmuseum, Hanover. 113 *Kairouan I*, 1914. Watercolour, $8\frac{1}{2} \times 10\frac{5}{8}$ (21·4 × 27). Staatsgalerie moderner Kunst, Munich. 115 *Promenade*, 1913. Oil on cardboard, $20 \times 22\frac{1}{2}$ (51 × 57). Städtische Galerie, Munich. 116 *Turkish Café II*, 1914. Oil on panel, $23\frac{5}{8} \times 14$ (60 × 35·5). Städtische Galerie, Munich.

MARC, FRANZ (1880–1916)
100 *Nude with Cat*, 1910. $34 \times 31\frac{1}{2}$ (86·5 × 80). Städtische Galerie, Munich. 101 *The Red Horses*, 1911. $47\frac{5}{8} \times 72$ (121 × 183). Paul E. Geier collection, Rome. 102 *Blue Horse I*, 1911. $44\frac{1}{8} \times 33\frac{1}{4}$ (112 × 84·5). Städtische Galerie, Munich. 103 *Red Roe Deer II*, 1912. $27\frac{1}{2} \times 39\frac{3}{8}$ (70 × 100). Staatsgalerie moderner Kunst, Munich. 104 *Tiger*, 1912. $43\frac{1}{4} \times 39\frac{3}{4}$ (110

× 101). Städtische Galerie, Munich. 105 *The Mandrill*, 1913. $35\frac{7}{8} \times 51\frac{1}{2}$ (91 × 131). Staatsgalerie moderner Kunst, Munich. 106 *Animal Fates*, 1913. $77\frac{1}{8} \times 104\frac{3}{4}$ (196 × 266). Kunstmuseum, Basle. 107 *Tyrol*, 1913–14. $53\frac{3}{8} \times 56\frac{7}{8}$ (135·7 × 144·5). Staatsgalerie moderner Kunst, Munich. 108 *Struggling Forms*, 1914. $35\frac{7}{8} \times 51\frac{3}{4}$ (91 × 131·5). Staatsgalerie moderner Kunst, Munich.

MEIDNER, LUDWIG (1884–1966)

137 *Self-portrait*, 1915. Pencil drawing, 23 × 18 (58·3 × 45·7). Staatsgalerie moderner Kunst, Munich. 138 *Apocalyptic Landscape*, c. 1913. $31\frac{1}{2} \times 77\frac{1}{8}$ (80 × 196). Nationalgalerie, Berlin.

MODERSOHN-BECKER, PAULA (1876–1907)

8 *Self-portrait with Amber Necklace*, c. 1906. $23\frac{5}{8} \times 19\frac{5}{8}$ (60 × 50). Roselius collection, Bremen. 9 *Nude Girl with Goldfish Bowl*, c. 1906. $41\frac{3}{8} \times 21\frac{1}{4}$ (105 × 54). Staatsgalerie moderner Kunst, Munich.

MORGNER, WILHELM (1891–1917)

158 *Astral Composition XIV*, 1912. Oil on cardboard, $29\frac{1}{2} \times 39\frac{3}{8}$ (75 × 100). Kunstmuseum, Düsseldorf.

MUELLER, OTTO (1874–1930)

52 *Two Girls in the Grass*. Tempera, $55\frac{1}{2} \times 43\frac{3}{8}$ (141 × 110). Staatsgalerie moderner Kunst, Munich (loan from L.G. Buchheim collection). 69 *The Judgment of Paris*, 1910–11. Tempera, $70\frac{1}{2} \times 48\frac{7}{8}$ (179 × 124). Galerie des XX. Jahrhunderts, Berlin. 70 *Three Nudes Before a Mirror*, c. 1912. Tempera, $59 \times 47\frac{1}{4}$ (150 × 120). Staatsgalerie moderner Kunst, Munich (loan from L.G. Buchheim collection). 71 *Couple in Bar*, c. 1922. Tempera, $42\frac{7}{8} \times 33\frac{7}{8}$ (109 × 86).

MÜNTER, GABRIELE (1877–1962)

93 *View of Murnau Moss*, 1908. Oil on cardboard, $12\frac{7}{8} \times 16$ (32·7 × 40·5). Städtische Galerie, Munich. 94 *Kandinsky*, 1906. Coloured woodcut, $9\frac{3}{4} \times 7$ (24·8 × 17·8). 96 *Still-life with St George*, 1911. Oil on cardboard, $20\frac{1}{8} \times 26\frac{3}{4}$ (51 × 68). Städtische Galerie, Munich.

NAUEN, HEINRICH (1880–1940)

155 *In the Garden*, 1913. Tempera on canvas, $82\frac{5}{8} \times 106\frac{1}{4}$ (210 × 270). Kaiser Wilhelm Museum, Krefeld. 156 *The Good Samaritan*, 1914. Tempera on paper, $66\frac{7}{8} \times 47\frac{1}{4}$ (170 × 120). Wallraf-Richartz Museum, Cologne.

NOLDE, EMIL (1867–1956)

50 *Tropical Sun*, 1914. $27\frac{1}{2} \times 41\frac{3}{4}$ (70 × 106). Ada and Emil Nolde Foundation, Seebüll. 51 *The Dance round the Golden Calf*, 1910. $34\frac{5}{8} \times 41\frac{3}{8}$ (88 × 105). Staatsgalerie moderner Kunst, Munich. 59 *In the Corn*, 1906. $25\frac{5}{8} \times 32\frac{1}{4}$ (65 × 82). Ada and Emil Nolde Foundation, Seebüll. 60 *Market People*, 1908. $28\frac{3}{4} \times 34\frac{5}{8}$ (73 × 88). Ada and Emil Nolde Foundation, Seebüll. 61 *The Last Supper*, 1909. $32\frac{5}{8} \times 41\frac{3}{4}$ (83 × 106). Ada and Emil Nolde Foundation, Seebüll. 62 *Hamburg, the Freihafen*, 1910. Etching, $12\frac{1}{8} \times 16\frac{1}{8}$ (30·8 × 41). 63 *Slovenes*, 1911. $31\frac{1}{8} \times 27\frac{1}{8}$ (79 × 69). 64 *Life of Christ: The Nativity*, 1911–12. $39\frac{3}{8} \times 33\frac{7}{8}$ (100 × 86). Ada and Emil Nolde Foundation, Seebüll. 65 *Family*, 1917. Woodcut, $9\frac{1}{2} \times 12\frac{5}{8}$ (24 × 32).

PECHSTEIN, MAX (1881–1955)

66 *Before the Storm*, 1910. $27\frac{7}{8} \times 29\frac{1}{2}$ (70·8 × 74·9). Staatsgalerie moderner Kunst, Munich. 67 *Summer in the Dunes*, 1911. $31\frac{1}{2} \times 41\frac{3}{8}$ (80 × 105). Frau Pechstein collection, Berlin. 68 *Horse Fair*, 1910. $27\frac{1}{8} \times 31\frac{1}{2}$ (69 × 80). Baron H.H. Thyssen-Bornemisza collection.

ROHLFS, CHRISTIAN (1849–1938)

150 *Return of the Prodigal Son*, 1914–15. Tempera on canvas, $39\frac{3}{8} \times 31\frac{1}{2}$ (100 × 80). Museum Folkwang, Essen. 157 *Red Roofs Beneath Trees*, 1913. Tempera on canvas, $31\frac{1}{2} \times 39\frac{3}{8}$ (80 × 100). Staatliche Kunsthalle, Karlsruhe.

SCHIELE, EGON (1890–1918)

149 *Embrace*, 1917. $39\frac{3}{8} \times 66\frac{7}{8}$ (100 × 170). Österreichische Galerie, Vienna. 151 *Self-portrait*, 1910. Pencil and tempera, $22 \times 14\frac{1}{2}$ (55·8 × 36·9). Albertina, Vienna. 152 *Death Agony*, 1912. $27\frac{1}{2} \times 31\frac{1}{2}$ (70 × 80). Staatsgalerie moderner Kunst, Munich. 153 *Landscape: Krumau*, 1916. $42\frac{7}{8} \times 54\frac{3}{8}$ (109 × 138). Neue Galerie, Wolfgang Gurlitt Museum, Linz. 154 *The Family*, 1917. Unfinished. $58\frac{5}{8} \times 63$ (149 × 160). Österreichische Galerie, Vienna.

SCHMIDT-ROTTLUFF, KARL (1884–1976)

12 *Berliner Strasse, Dresden*, 1909. Lithograph, $16\frac{1}{2} \times 13\frac{3}{8}$ (42 × 34). 43 *Farmyard near Dangast*, 1910. $34 \times 37\frac{1}{4}$ (86·5 × 94·5). Galerie des XX. Jahrhunderts, Berlin. 44 *Lighthouse*, 1909. Watercolour, $26\frac{1}{8} \times 19\frac{1}{2}$ (66·4 × 49·5). L.G. Buchheim collection, Feldafing. 45 *Norwegian Landscape (Skrygedal)*, 1911. $34\frac{1}{4} \times 38\frac{3}{8}$ (87 × 97·5) Staatsgalerie moderner Kunst, Munich (loan from L.G. Buchheim collection). 46 *Summer*, 1913. $34\frac{5}{8} \times 41$ (88 × 104). Landesmuseum, Hanover. 47 *Houses at Night*, 1912. $37\frac{5}{8} \times 34$ (95·5 × 86·5). M. Rauert collection, Hamburg. 48 *Pharisees*, 1912. $29\frac{7}{8} \times 44\frac{1}{8}$ (76 × 112). The Museum of Modern Art, New York. 49 *Woman Resting*, 1912. $29\frac{5}{8} \times 33\frac{1}{8}$ (76 × 84). Staatsgalerie moderner Kunst, Munich. 53 *Autumn Landscape*, 1913. $34\frac{1}{4} \times 37\frac{3}{8}$ (87 × 95). Staatsgalerie moderner Kunst, Munich (loan from L.G. Buchheim collection). 54 *Mourners on the Beach*, 1914. Woodcut, $15\frac{1}{2} \times 19\frac{5}{8}$ (39·4 × 49·8). 55 *Portrait of a Girl*, 1915. $38\frac{3}{4} \times 24$ (98·5 × 61). Staatsgalerie moderner Kunst, Munich (loan from L.G. Buchheim collection). 56 *Has Not Christ Appeared to You?*, 1918. Woodcut, $19\frac{5}{8} \times 15\frac{3}{8}$ (50 × 39). 57 *Conversation about Death*, 1920. $44\frac{1}{8} \times 38\frac{3}{8}$ (112 × 97·5). Staatsgalerie moderner Kunst, Munich (loan from M. Kruss collection). 58 *Woman in the Forest*, 1920. Watercolour, $15\frac{7}{8} \times 20\frac{1}{8}$ (40·3 × 51·1). L.G. Buchheim collection, Feldafing.

UHDE, FRITZ VON (1848–1911)

4 *Two Girls in a Garden*, 1892. $57\frac{1}{4} \times 46\frac{1}{4}$ (145·5 × 117). Neue Pinakothek, Munich.

WEREFKIN, MARIANNE (1870–1938)

74 *Self-portrait*, c. 1908. Oil on cardboard, $20 \times 13\frac{3}{8}$ (51 × 34). Städtische Galerie, Munich.

Italic figures are illustration numbers. **Index**